God's Treasure System

LEARNING TO VALUE WHAT GOD VALUES

SHANNON B. STEUERWALD

THE IRONWOOD TOOLBOOK SERIES

The Ironwood Toolbook Series is designed to address specific facets of ministry and to provide practical instruction in areas such as leadership, management, counseling, team building, youth work, music, and service ministries. The tried and tested contents of this series, an integral part of Ironwood, are now available to assist individuals and ministries. To God alone be the glory for the countless hours of service that have made this series possible.

Unless otherwise noted, Scripture quotations are from the Authorized King James Version.

For information concerning the Ironwood Toolbook Series or any other resources listed in this book, contact us at www.ironwood.org.

Editor: Beneth Perry
Cover Design: Allison Pust, Sarah Forsythe
Content Layout: Allison Pust, Sarah Forsythe

Iron Sharpeneth Iron Publications
Newberry Springs, California

Chapter 1: Treasure Hunting.............................11

Chapter 2: A Virtuous Woman..........................23

Chapter 3: The Trials of Our Faith....................37

Chapter 4: Marriage.......................................53

Chapter 5: God's Promises...............................69

Chapter 6: His Lovingkindness........................87

Chapter 7: The Death of a Saint..................... 103

Chapter 8: A Meek and Quiet Spirit................ 125

Chapter 9: Wisdom...................................... 141

Chapter 10: The Work of Christ...................... 153

Epilogue: The System's Foundation................. 167

Appendix A: Entertaining God's Values........... 171

Appendix B: A Parallel of God's Kindness........ 175

Appendix C: Lest I Forget the Gospel's Value in My Life 181

Appendix D: Treasuring God's Kindness 185

Appendix E: As unto the Lord....................... 187

Appendix F: Summary of the Treasures........... 191

Notes 197

Table of Contents

To my parents Walt and Betty Brock

Thank you for valuing what God values and for teaching those eternal values to me. Thank you for showing me that dipping into God's treasure chest is never risky or disappointing. Thank you for sharing God's treasure map, the Bible, and for teaching me how to read and apply it.

Dedication

To my husband and children:
Thank you for allowing me to do what I love to do . . . be your homemaker plus serve by your side in ministry. God really does give us the desires of our hearts. I love you all. Thank you for loving me.

To my Sunday school class:
Much of what is in this book was first presented to you. I love teaching, and I love learning. Thank you for allowing me to share with you what God has been teaching me. I hope and pray we continue learning together.

To my editorial friends and family:
Thank you for taking time out of your busy schedules to read this book when it still needed some fine tuning. I especially want to thank Brina Kemlo and Christy Hendricks for their honest critiquing and helpful suggesting. My dad Walt Brock and my brother David Brock were well-qualified editors in making sure I got it right. Thank you.

I am grateful to my pastor Ron Perry and his wife Beneth for being worthy editors of this book and loving leaders in my life.

Acknowledgements

Dear Readers,

The dictionary definition of *system* means "an arrangement of things so connected as to form a unity or organic whole; a set of principles." We call the galaxy of stars above us the solar system, even though scientists discover new things each day about the solar system. In the same way, I call God's values a treasure system, even though each week I discover new truths about His treasure system. I use the word *system* because the treasures covered in the following chapters do have a connection to each other, although you may not have seen the connection before reading this book. This study is not exhaustive; it is, I hope and pray, a beginning for you as it was for me. When scientists discover a new star in the galaxy, they name it, study it, and then add it to the solar system. When you learn a new thing that God values, I hope you will name it, study it, and then add that value to God's treasure system so that you can begin to reap the benefits of valuing what God values.

I know that my personal relationship with Christ, my parenting skills, my work ethic, my faithfulness and service to my local church, and my marriage only improve as I value and then apply the principles set forth in God's treasure system. The compilation of principles found in this book is not meant to be digested all at once. Although a part of me wishes this book would be a "can't-put-it-down" type of book, I know this is unrealistic.

Whether you read this book for personal spiritual growth or you use this book as a springboard in your own teaching opportunities, I trust you will grasp the importance of choosing to value what God values.

All for Him,
Shannon B. Steuerwald
2 Timothy 1:12

Letter to Readers

Foreword

I was extremely honored when my daughter asked me to write the foreword for her new book. As we are "bringing up" our children in the "nurture and admonition of the Lord" (Ephesians 6:4), we never know what one little attitude, comment, or action will create a lasting impression, an impression so strong that it can and often does permanently influence that child's life. In writing this book, which is basically about thinking like God thinks when it comes to what is valuable and important in life, Shannon has obviously picked up on something that is now two generations strong in our family. My parents had a small plaque on the wall in the back hallway of their home which I saw every time I went in and out of the house. The words of that plaque left an indelible mark on my mind, which in turn created an attitude and eventual action in my life.

> Only one life
> 'Twill soon be past,
> Only what's done
> For Christ will last.
> --Author unknown

Years later in the formative years of our children's lives, my wife put that same quote on the wall right beside the door we all went in and out of many times a day.

As you read this book on the importance of cherishing what God values and thinking eternally while living in a temporal world, may each treasure become personally yours. In observing Shannon and her husband Steve going about the constant challenge of bringing up their own children and actively serving in ministry for the Lord, I see a couple who are living out what is written in this book. Its basic premise and the subject of each chapter are trustworthy not only because they are biblically correct but also because they are authenticated by the eternal values modeled in their home.

To my daughter I say, "Great job, Shannon!" To the reader I say that I trust you will be as challenged as I was to evaluate my thought patterns by God's treasure system.—*Walt Brock*

Treasure Hunting 1

Isaiah 40:8

The grass withereth, the flower fadeth:
but the word of our God shall stand for ever.

As children, my brothers and I had fun burying a treasure and drawing a map so that we could find the treasure at a later date. Our treasures—scrap metal, broken appliances, and Monopoly money—were important items to us. We spent many hours pretending to be treasure hunters. Because for us, finding treasures was a great adventure, we assumed others would enjoy it, too.

We soon discovered what other people treasured, and we found great pleasure in confiscating those precious items. I grew up at Ironwood, a Christian camp in the high desert of California. For many of the summer staff members, shoes became a precious item, because the desert sand would heat up and become a danger to bare feet. But for us pygmies (a nickname given to us staff children), who had been running around barefoot in the desert for some time, our feet became calloused to the hot sand; and therefore, shoes were not precious to us at all: we did not value them or consider them important. As a matter of fact, they were downright a bother to us. Once we found out how "precious" shoes were to the adult workers at camp, we began to confiscate their shoes. Summer staff members began complaining about their shoes disappearing. We were not named desert pygmies without reason. We could "steal" shoes and be confident that the adults would not chase us into the sand with their bare feet. After much pleading and bartering (or once our parents told us it was time to stop), we would give a roughly drawn map to the shoeless staff members so that they could find their buried "treasures."

Those were fun days. They are now happy memories.

What we pygmies quickly realized was that what we considered important (broken appliances) just was not important to the adults, and that what the adults considered important (shoes) just was not important to us. So, for the hunt to be successful, we grabbed shoes and hid them, knowing that these treasured items were so valuable to the owner that he would hunt hard for them. The strategy worked well, and we enjoyed many memorable hours watching staff members search for their hidden shoes.

Now that I am grown and have children of my own, I have observed that treasure hunting is not an oddity unique only to my childhood. I find my children's treasures buried in the bottom of closets or in small holes around our yard or displayed for months on top of a cluttered dresser with other not-so-fashionable keepsakes. My son Devon had a pair of binoculars that were his treasure for quite a long time. The only problem was that these binoculars, specially made by his great-grandma, were really two empty toilet paper rolls taped together and decorated with special designs drawn all over the cardboard rolls. He stored this treasure in all kinds of places until before long, he had stepped on them, rolled over them, and spilled something on them. We eventually threw the homemade binoculars away only to find out that Great-Grandma had made him a new pair. Devon has now outgrown the preciousness of his handmade memento; but while the binoculars were important to him, he kept them close to him at all times.

More Than a Child's Fantasy

We all have treasures in our lives, things and people we value. Memories we store in keepsakes. Hobbies we put time and energy into. Careers we pursue. Children we rear. Marriages we invest in. Money we save. Food we eat. Possessions we purchase. Heroes we follow. Books we read. Churches we attend. Games we play. Information we research. Relationships we restore. Sleep we crave. The God we worship. Entertainment we view. Education we receive. All or some of these areas listed can be and probably are treasures to us. I look at the list and can name a few items that I value—some are worthy of treasuring and some are not.

How do we know when something is valuable to us? Time is usually the answer. I treasure the things I invest the most time in. When I get up each morning, I begin my treasure hunt: my heart determines what is of value, my mind maps out the route to find the treasure, and my body starts hunting, digging, investing in, protecting, and displaying my treasure. Time equals value. When I invest time, I am giving the object of my time value. If I value my children, I will spend time with them. If I value my job, I will invest time in my job. If I value my church, I will spend time in my church. If I value my friends, I will give them my time. What we do with our time determines what we value, what we treasure.

To illustrate, I will make a confession. I treasure ice cream. How do I know I treasure ice cream? I have made it a priority. For instance, I refuse to go on any diet that does not allow me the pleasure of ice cream. Just to prove that I could diet and eat ice cream, I maintained a weight loss program where I could lose weight while indulging in my ice cream. Every night after my children were in bed and the house was quiet, I would enjoy a bowl of ice cream. Craving ice cream is a part of my heritage, mostly from my grandpa who loved his ice cream, too. I am not saying that this evening ritual is a good one; I am just admitting that I treasure ice cream so much that I say no to certain foods and yes to more exercise so that I can enjoy that one bowl of ice cream each night. As a matter of fact, I am willing to exercise an extra half hour in order to eat a bowl of ice cream. I realize that exercise is helping me beyond just keeping the weight off while enjoying ice cream, and I justify eating the ice cream by telling myself that dairy products are good for my bones. But when I shave away the justifications, reality sinks in and I confess that I treasure ice cream. I value ice cream, and I spend time during my day earning the right to eat my bowl of ice cream.

We all have treasures that we spend time hunting for, obtaining, and valuing. The company Ebay exists because people enjoy treasure hunting. Treasure hunting is not just a child's fantasy; treasure hunting is an adult activity, too. If we took the time to evaluate what is important to us by mapping out our steps of the last week, we all would be able to draw a map of our lives that leads us to our treasures.

The Worth of a Treasure
When we receive a valuable necklace with a rare jewel, we do not by nature hang it on our front door knob for the world to see and admire. Why? Because the jewel would be exposed to bad weather and thieves. Because we are careful to protect costly items, we place them in fireproof safe boxes or bank vaults. But what is valuable to me may not be valuable to another. So we have to ask ourselves what makes an item irreplaceable.

My grandmother gave me a simulated pearl necklace that is not valuable by an assessor's opinion, but it is priceless to me because the necklace is part of my heritage and because my grandmother valued the necklace. Things do not have to come with a high price tag to be valuable. A vase may be valuable because it is fragile. A truck may be valuable because it is durable. A painting may be valuable because it is an original, although faded. A diamond may be valuable because it shines. A book may be valuable because of its publication date. A tool may be valuable because it is useful. A piece of pottery may be valuable because of its potter. A house may be valuable because of its location. A necklace may be valuable because of its original owner. We declare items valuable based on many variables.

For the majority of our items, though, we view whether a treasure is valuable or not based on just a few basic variables. Only one variable needs to hit a chord with our heart for us to deem an item valuable.

- Its Origin: Where did it come from? Who made it?
- Its Use: Why was it made? What is the significance of its creation? How was it used?
- Its Potential: What are my returns if I sell it? Can I make more later if I save it? Does it benefit me to store it?

I have to remember, though, that no matter how valuable an item is on earth, there is more to my life than my earthly treasures. If this were not true, the richest people in the world would be the happiest, most content people alive. But through my observations, they are not; furthermore, when I have asked wealthy people what makes them happy, the answer they give me is not their money or possessions. There is more to life than earthly treasures.

Jesus wanted His disciples to be mindful of the danger of storing up temporal treasures for personal gain.

> Matthew 6:19-21—Lay not up for yourselves treasures upon earth, where moth and rust doth corrupt, and where thieves break through and steal: But lay up for yourselves treasures in heaven, where neither

moth nor rust doth corrupt, and where thieves do not break through nor steal: For where your treasure is, there will your heart be also.

Jesus mentions two problems with spending too much time accumulating earthly treasures: eventually the treasure gets rusty and falls apart, and a thief could steal the treasure. The three-wheeler I treasured as a child eventually lost its front wheel, making it almost useless (except for popping wheelies down steep hills). Eventually the plastic rotted from the sun, and the three-wheeler went to the dump. I have friends who have been robbed, and I have observed that those experiences are not easy for them to get over. Possessions were lost and emotions were frazzled. Earthly treasures fade; some are stolen. They do not last forever.

Jesus' solution to the high-risk, low-return of our earthly treasures is simple: we need to spend our time hunting down and obtaining heavenly treasures, because those treasures do not rust, do not fall apart, and cannot be stolen. Why waste time and money seeking treasures that fall apart, when God tells us of treasures that last forever? These treasures are priceless, eternal, and abundant. When I invest in these treasures, they follow me to heaven! All of the variables point directly to the fact that these heavenly treasures are precious and worthy of my investment.

God's Treasure Map

I want to know where I can find the heavenly treasures God speaks of. If God calls something or someone *precious*, I then need to agree with His value system and invest my time in finding and possessing those treasures. To learn about the location of these treasures, we need a treasure map.

The words *treasure map* perk my interest. Drawing treasure maps was really fun when I was a child. Now, as a parent, I still find enjoyment in helping my children bury a "treasure" and then draw a map to it. Sometimes the maps are accurate; other times, we never find the buried treasure. God's treasure map will never send me down the wrong trail.

The Bible is God's treasure map because it outlines for us how we can find these heavenly treasures that cannot rust or be stolen. The heavenly treasures Christ speaks of in the Gospel of Matthew are those treasures that God has declared to be precious in His sight. They will not rust; they will not be stolen. These treasures are not things we naturally desire and value; as a matter of fact, we Christians possess many of these treasures at the moment of our salvation but fail to value them as we should.

In God's treasure map, the Bible, God often tells us what our returns are for investing in and valuing His treasures. Just as my grandmother's pearl necklace is not valuable because of its financial worth but rather because my grandmother valued it, we need to realize that God's treasure system does not come with great earthly, financial gains. Rather, we need to learn to value His treasure system because He says these things are valuable to Him. His spoken declaration of value should be enough for us to seek these treasures.

God's map is not hard to follow, but following the map does involve some searching on our part. God does not want His treasures to be a mystery; but He knows that if we value what He values, we will follow the treasure map, obtain His treasures, declare those treasures precious because of God's assessment, not man's, and begin valuing God's treasure system as outlined in the Bible.

This investment in God's treasure system has no risk involved, but the treasure is not free. Treasures have costs—some greater than others—but all have a price tag. According to God's system, the returns far outweigh the cost involved, as we will discover in our study of each treasure.

Obviously, we will need God's treasure map to hunt for God's treasures. Without the map, we have no hope of finding the treasure. We can be confident that God's Word is a sure thing. Unlike my attempts at drawing treasure maps, there are no false clues or faulty steps in God's treasure map. The Bible is authentic. If we follow it, we will always find the treasure.

God's treasure map is the real thing and worthy of trusting.

> Proverbs 30:5—Every word of God is pure: he is a shield unto them that put their trust in him.

2 Samuel 22:31—As for God, his way is perfect; the word of the LORD is tried: he is a buckler to all them that trust in him.

God's treasure map—whether written or spoken—is a sure investment with a history of great gains with eternal values.

Acts 6:7—And the word of God increased; and the number of the disciples multiplied in Jerusalem greatly; and a great company of the priests were obedient to the faith.

Acts 12:24—But the word of God grew and multiplied.

Acts 19:20—So mightily grew the word of God and prevailed.

God's treasure map outlines the path and becomes a weapon to fight the enemies that attempt to thwart the treasure hunt.

Ephesians 6:17—And take the helmet of salvation, and the sword of the Spirit, which is the word of God.

Psalm 119:105—Thy word is a lamp unto my feet, and a light unto my path.

God's treasure map is alive and powerful and can guide our hearts to its truths.

Hebrews 4:12—For the word of God is quick, and powerful, and sharper than any twoedged sword, piercing even to the dividing asunder of soul and spirit, and of the joints and marrow, and is a discerner of the thoughts and intents of the heart.

God's treasure map abides forever; there is no risk to the map changing or being destroyed.

1 Peter 1:23—Being born again, not of corruptible seed, but of incorruptible, by the word of God, which liveth and abideth for ever.

Isaiah 40:8—The grass withereth, the flower fadeth: but the word of our God shall stand for ever.

God's treasure map not only leads us to His treasures but also is itself a treasure to be valued and desired.

> Psalm 19:7-11—The law of the LORD is perfect, converting the soul: the testimony of the LORD is sure, making wise the simple. The statutes of the LORD are right, rejoicing the heart: the commandment of the LORD is pure, enlightening the eyes. The fear of the LORD is clean, enduring for ever: the judgments of the LORD are true and righteous altogether. More to be desired are they than gold, yea, than much fine gold: sweeter also than honey and the honeycomb. Moreover by them is thy servant warned: and in keeping of them there is great reward.

God also describes His Word as enriching rain (Isaiah 55:10-11), a fruitful seed (1 Peter 1:23), a piercing sword (Ephesians 6:17; Hebrews 4:12; Revelation 19:11-21), a refining fire (Jeremiah 23:23-29), a forceful hammer (Jeremiah 23:29), an illuminating lamp (Psalm 119:105, 130; Proverbs 6:23; 2 Peter 1:19), a revealing and reflecting mirror (James 1:22-25; 2 Corinthians 3:18), cleansing water (Ephesians 5:26-27; John 15:3; Psalm 119:9-11), pure silver (Psalm 12:6), and nourishing milk and sustaining meat (1 Corinthians 3:2; 1 Peter 2:2).

If I am to go on a treasure hunt where I know Satan is going to do his best to destroy my goals and discourage my resolve, what better tool to possess than a treasure map that gives me not only the clues to finding God's treasure but also the weaponry, the light, the heat, and the nourishment I need to sustain and protect me on my treasure hunt. I would be foolish to think that I could find heavenly treasures without the Bible, God's treasure map!

God's Treasure System
Warning! In the chapters to follow, we will discover that what is precious in God's sight and what should then be precious in our sight is not going to make sense to the natural man. We will not become wealthy by the world's standard, but we will be spiritually wealthy by possessing and valuing the very elements that God considers to be precious in His sight.

Just as God told the prophet Isaiah, "For my thoughts are not your thoughts, neither are your ways my ways" (Isaiah 55:8), we have to assume that God's treasure system is not naturally our treasure system. This truth does not change the fact that our treasure system should align with God's. This study outlines God's treasure system so that we can apply this new-found knowledge of God to our lives.

I have a heavenly Father Who desires for me to value what He values. God desires that we look forward to spending time with Him. The more I spend time with Him, the more I learn of Him and begin to understand what He values, what He considers precious, what He wants of me, what He loves, and, in turn, what I should value, what I should consider precious, what I should desire to do for Him, and what I should love. After all, He is my heavenly Father; and as His child, I so much want to emulate His treasure system in my life. When children and teenagers ask me why they should spend time with the Lord by reading the Bible and praying, my answer is simply that we will not become like Christ unless we spend time getting to know Christ. If we truly value our relationship with God, we will spend the time nurturing the relationship. His values will become our values proportionally to the time we spend with Him.

Which brings us to the final point before we begin our treasure hunt: this expedition is useless to us if we do not first value God. Knowing what God treasures will not transform our lives unless we first value God. This study becomes a good starting point to getting to know God more. I have found through personal experience that the more I know of God, the more I trust Him; and the more I trust Him, the more I find Him to be faithful.

So, with God's treasure map to guide us, we begin our treasure hunt of God's values. I trust each of us will learn to value the treasures of God.

Dear Reader,

What I am about to request is unusual for authors to do, but I believe is necessary for the full impact of your understanding of *God's Treasure System*. You have just finished chapter 1; now I want you to flip all the way to the back of the book to the last chapter and read chapter 10 before returning to chapter 2. I then want you to promise yourself that after reading chapters 2 through 9, you will conclude reading this book by again reading chapter 10. God's treasure system pivots on the treasure talked of in chapter 10. If there is one chapter I wish for you to read over and over again, it would be chapter 10.

So, as the author, I give you permission to read the last chapter first! Enjoy.

Shannon B. Steuerwald

Proverbs 31:10

Who can find a virtuous woman? for her price is far above rubies.

Confession time . . . I have dreaded Sunday school classes or Bible studies that take me back to Proverbs 31. This response is sinful, and I have often found myself going to God for forgiveness. I found my brain "shutting down" any time I heard a reference to Proverbs 31 because that chapter seemed to outline a very busy woman whose husband sat all day at the gates. I had a poor perspective and a sinful response to this most needful area in my life.

I did not understand how the truths of Philippians 4, where I was commanded to think on virtue, had anything to do with Proverbs 31, where a lady seemed too busy to do anything but think about tilling the ground and sewing clothes for her children. For many years, I was confused about what being a virtuous woman meant according to Proverbs 31, until I became one of those Sunday school teachers who studied Proverbs 31 in preparation for teaching about virtue. I realized through my studies that I did not understand the Philippians 4 and Proverbs 31 correlation because there really was not one. *Virtue* in Philippians 4 refers to morality, and *virtue* in Proverbs 31 refers to strength.

Defining Virtue Properly

Virtue as it is rendered in Proverbs is an Old English word that according to Noah Webster's *1828 Dictionary* has a primary meaning of "strength from straining, stretching, or extending." Webster goes on to say that the first three definitions of *virtue* are 1) "strength," which we apply as the inner quality that makes one strong; 2) "bravery," which we seldom use today as a meaning of *virtue*; and 3) "moral goodness," which is today's most commonly used definition of virtue, often referring to the moral excellence in one's character and practice.[1]

When God tells us in Philippians 4:8 to think on things that are virtuous, He commands us to think on things that are morally sound and worthy of praise and glory. When 2 Peter 1:3 tells us that we are called to glory and virtue, we can claim the promise that God has given us what we need to be morally good and excellent. When Peter exhorts us in 2 Peter 1:5 to add to our faith virtue, we are commanded to grow and build on our faith by following after what is morally good and what is worthy of praise. All of the uses of *virtue* in these passages relate to moral goodness, moral excellence, glory, and praise. [2]

But when Proverbs 31 tells us that a virtuous woman is priceless, God is not saying that a morally excellent woman is priceless. Furthermore, when Proverbs 12:4a says, "A virtuous woman is a crown to her husband," God is not saying that a morally good woman is a crown to her husband. The virtue of Proverbs 31 is most closely related to Webster's first definition of strength of character.

The word *virtuous* of Proverbs 31 and Proverbs 12:4 means a force, possessing might and power, being active, showing strength. [3] This same word is translated in the Old Testament using words such as *army, host, wealth, force, substance, valor, able, valiantly, strength, and power*. The Latin background of the word *virtus* where we derive *virtue* implies manly strength and power. [4]

In Proverbs 31, King Lemuel, whom scholars believe to be King Solomon, is sharing some of the lessons his mother Bathsheba taught him. We know Bathsheba's story of falling and being forgiven, and we have read of her fortitude in protecting her son's kingship. We now read her advice to Solomon. Bathsheba begins her advice in Proverbs 31 by telling Solomon to "give not thy strength unto women" (Proverbs 31:3). The word *strength* in this verse is the same word as *virtuous* in verse 10: "who can find a virtuous woman." Bathsheba warns Solomon not to give his strength and power to a woman, but then tells him that an able woman of valor and strength is precious. We can conclude, then, that being virtuous is not just a trait for women to possess and value. In the following verses, the phrases in quotation marks are the same Hebrew word for *virtuous* in Proverbs 31.
- Ruth 2:1 describes Boaz as a "mighty man of wealth."
- 1 Samuel 16:18 describes David as a "valiant man."
- 1 Kings 11:28 describes Jeroboam as a "mighty man of valour."
- 2 Kings 5:1 describes Naaman as a "mighty man in valour."

- 1 Chronicles 9:13 describes the men in charge of the house of God as "able men."
- Ruth 3:11 describes Ruth as a "virtuous woman."

Men *and* women need to be virtuous—to be strong and valiant. We need to possess that inner strength of character Webster describes when defining *virtue*.

Women of Manly Strength

The God-inspired truth of Proverbs 31:10 says that God sees a virtuous woman as a treasure that is worth more than rubies. Rubies, a valuable coral from the Mediterranean or a valuable pearl, were precious commodities to the people of Solomon's day. Precious stones were treasures, and a virtuous woman was worth more, far more, than these stones.

Now comes the difficult question: does God really treasure a woman of manly strength and power? Is God asking women to lift weights to be strong like a man or to enter the workforce and rise to power in order to fulfill the Proverbs 31 mandate?

In order to answer these questions, I studied the context of the word *virtue* in other Bible passages to get a better understanding of its meaning. Oftentimes, the word was used to rally armies to be valiant in time of battle or to gather hosts of people for a mighty undertaking. When I read Proverbs 31 in light of this knowledge, I found that this woman had a huge undertaking in caring for her family. Instead of being inactive, complaining, or distracted, she was active, strong, and powerful in her pursuit of caring for her family. In essence, she took the mandate of being a keeper of the home very seriously. She rallied her family and prepared them for the spiritual battles ahead while caring for their physical and emotional needs. She led and cared for her family by example. This servant leadership required an inner strength that made her able to do the physical and emotional tasks.

Webster's primary definition of virtue implies that this character quality grows or increases with "stretching," a kind of stretching that properly responds to the strains and pressures of life. This kind of inner strength will only get stronger in the face of adversity. A virtuous woman by definition is a woman who possesses an inner strength of character that produces outward manifestations of strength and character.

Herbert Lockyer finds eight characteristics in Proverbs 31 that define a virtuous woman.[5] These characteristics are the outward manifestations of a woman that possesses virtue.

She is industrious.
Proverbs 31:13—She worketh willingly with her hands.
Proverbs 31:15—She riseth also while it is yet night, and giveth meat to her household.
Proverbs 31:16—With the fruit of her hands she planteth a vineyard.
Proverbs 31:18—Her candle goeth not out by night.
Proverbs 31:19— She layeth her hands to the spindle, and her hands hold the distaff.
Proverbs 31:27—She . . . eateth not the bread of idleness.

She is self-disciplined.
Proverbs 31:15—She riseth also while it is yet night, and giveth meat to her household.
Proverbs 31:17—She girdeth her loins with strength, and strengtheneth her arms.

She is orderly.
Proverbs 31:15—She riseth also while it is yet night, and giveth meat to her household, and a portion to her maidens.
Proverbs 31:21—She is not afraid of the snow for her household: for all her household are clothed with scarlet.
Proverbs 31:27—She looketh well to the ways of her household.

She is business-minded.
Proverbs 31:14—She is like the merchants' ships; she bringeth her food from afar.
Proverbs 31:16—She considereth a field, and buyeth it: with the fruit of her hands she planteth a vineyard.
Proverbs 31:18—She perceiveth that her merchandise is good.
Proverbs 31:19a—She layeth her hands to the spindle.

Proverbs 31:24—She maketh fine linen, and selleth it; and delivereth girdles unto the merchant.

She is refined in taste and style.
Proverbs 31:21—All her household are clothed with scarlet.
Proverbs 31:22— She maketh herself coverings of tapestry; her clothing is silk and purple.
Proverbs 31:25—Strength and honour are her clothing.

She is hospitable.
Proverbs 31:15—She giveth meat to her household, and a portion to her maidens.
Proverbs 31:20—She stretcheth out her hand to the poor; yea, she reacheth forth her hands to the needy.
Proverbs 31:26—In her tongue is the law of kindness.

She is charitable.
Proverbs 31:12—She will do him good and not evil all the days of her life.
Proverbs 31:15—She giveth meat to her household, and a portion to her maidens.
Proverbs 31:20—She stretcheth out her hand to the poor; yea, she reacheth forth her hands to the needy.

She is spiritually-minded.
Proverbs 31:25—Strength and honour are her clothing; and she shall rejoice in time to come.
Proverbs 31:26—She openeth her mouth with wisdom; and in her tongue is the law of kindness.
Proverbs 31:30—Favour is deceitful, and beauty is vain: but a woman that feareth the LORD, she shall be praised.

In order for a woman to be diligent in the duties of keeping her home, she needs to possess those characteristics. After studying this chapter, I no longer picture a woman who is running haggardly from one chore to the next. Instead, I see a woman who finds pleasure in taking care of her family. I see a woman who is courageous and diligent in her responsibilities. I see a family that views their home as a haven because of the labors of the virtuous matriarch in the home. The pressures of life did not tear down this woman, because her inner strength from God gave her greater abilities and a stronger determination to do what God had asked her to do.

Treasures Close to Home

I know a woman who is more valuable than any rare or priceless jewel that I could ever possess. Actually, I have a few women in my life that exhibit virtuous characteristics. Both of my grandmothers were valiant, strong women. I thank God often for the heritage He has given me as a result of their testimony and commitment to doing what is right.

All of my life I have been exposed to a rare treasure. I did not know how rare this treasure was until later in life, nor did I treat this treasure with as much honor as was deserved. Now that I am older and maybe slightly wiser, I now know without a doubt that my mom is a treasure that is rare in Christian circles and virtually non-existent in the world. When I read Proverbs 31, I picture my mom. I see my mom rising early or staying up late, preparing food for her family, planning ahead, managing the budget, looking for good deals, teaching her children, paying attention to her physical health, sewing and mending clothes for her family, giving to those in need, reaching out to her neighbors, dressing appropriately, speaking wise words, listening to her children, supporting her husband in ministry, showing kindness to her children and husband, and fearing God.

When I look at the characteristics of a virtuous woman, I cannot think of one that my mom fails to exhibit. I know she would be quick to disagree with me, but I would expect that of her because she is spiritually-minded and realizes all she is and has is of God. I treasure my mom, not because of how she looks, how she cooks, or even how she loves me. I treasure her because she is virtuous. My mom chose to value what God values by seeking to be virtuous. I treasure the work that God did and continues to do in my mom's life.

Dear Mom,

You are a treasure from God. Thank you for saying yes to God and no to self so that I could grow up in a home filled with joy and security. You are a virtuous woman, and I now rise to the virtuous challenge in hopes that I, too, will consistently say yes to God and no to self so that my children will want to rise to the same godly challenge. I want the inner strength that is manifest in your life daily. I want to be like you because I see Christ in and through you.

You are real, Mom. There is nothing fake about you. I am thrilled to be your daughter, and honored. God is good. God is gracious. To Him be the glory.

I love you.
Shannon

Teaching the Principle of Virtue to My Children

Whether we are men or women, young or old, married or single, we can apply this treasure in our lives. Some people may believe that because the example of a virtuous woman in Proverbs 31 is so clearly a married woman with children, then being a virtuous woman, a woman of inner strength, is only a married mother's responsibility. I disagree. A virtuous woman is any woman—married, single, young, old, or widowed. I need to apply this passage not only to myself but also to my daughter. One of the best ways that I can treasure a virtuous woman like God treasures one, besides becoming one myself, is to do all I can to make sure that my own offspring value a virtuous woman.

I want my boys to grow up desiring to marry a virtuous woman. I want them to know how a virtuous woman looks, acts, talks, and thinks. I want them to know how the opposite of a virtuous woman (a strange woman) looks, acts, talks, and thinks. I want to do all I can to teach them the eternal benefits of choosing a virtuous woman instead of the strange woman described in Proverbs. My job as their mother is to teach my boys the treasure of a virtuous woman so clearly that the strange woman described in Proverbs 5 and 7 is disgustingly ugly to them, while the virtuous woman is a prize to be sought and earned. If my husband and I fail to teach our boys to value what God values, they very easily could make poor choices with devastating consequences that follow them the rest of their adult years.

Not only do I need to teach my boys to value a woman who is virtuous, I also want my daughter to grow up desiring to be a virtuous woman. I want to surround her with positive examples of virtuous women. I want her to want to be like them. I want her to believe that the strange women of Proverbs have nothing to offer her, and I want to show her the benefits of being virtuous. This means that my example in the home will be important to her overall acceptance of this treasure. By example, I need to be a hard worker in our home; I need to be self-disciplined in my habits and use of time; I need to be orderly in how I run our household and teach the importance of preparation; I need to be business-minded and teach important money and goal-setting principles; I need to be appropriate in how I dress and creative in how I decorate; I need to be hospitable, and open our home to others; I need to be charitable and give of my time, possessions, and money; I need to be spiritually-minded and choose God's ways over mine. And I need to do all of these with a joyful attitude that communicates to my daughter the joy of serving others and obeying God.

I desperately want my sons and daughter to value this treasure. I use the word *desperately* purposefully. I do not just want it. I desperately want it. But I do not think I want it enough when I pause and evaluate my prayer life, my priorities, and my personal example to my children in our home. I need to pray for my children more. I need to ask for God's grace and help. I need to realign my priorities and recall how important this treasure is in my life and in my children's lives. My dependence on God is crucial, and it is the best indicator to my children of my own spiritual relationship with God. My children need to know that I am leaning heavily on God while working diligently to be a godly parent.

Teaching our children what God values is a team effort. The older women need to teach the younger women. The older men need to teach the younger men. This principle is taught in Titus 2. Church members—single, married, or widowed—need to teach by example. Fathers need to communicate an honor system by treating their wives and daughters with value and by teaching their sons what makes a woman beautiful and precious. We all need to work together in teaching our children to value what God values. Our children *desperately* need us to value virtue.

Treasuring What God Treasures

If God treasures a virtuous woman, then we had better get busy in becoming a virtuous woman. Nothing of value comes easily. Just as the treasure of salvation cost Christ His life, so the treasure of a virtuous woman will cost us something.

When I began to ponder the characteristics of a virtuous woman, I first had to ask myself, "Do I really want to be virtuous?" Being industrious, self-disciplined, orderly, business-minded, refined, hospitable, charitable, and spiritually-minded are not easy challenges. Some, if not all, are downright impossible without God's help. [6]

Which leads me to the next question . . .

If the answer to my first question is "Yes, I want to be a virtuous woman," then the next question that naturally follows is, "How do I become a virtuous woman?" The answer is found in God's Word. I wish becoming a woman of virtue was as easy as taking twenty paces west, five paces south, and three feet down; but that is not how God operates. If becoming virtuous is all about *what I have to accomplish* and God is left behind in my pursuit for this treasure, then I would fail each time in my quest to become virtuous. Becoming virtuous starts first with my desiring to possess virtue and proceeds to my depending on God to give me His inner strength of character.

We see women who are trying to be virtuous on their own; and they soon crash and burn from exhaustion, stress, anger, and resentment. God never intended for a woman to be haggard while fulfilling her duties as a wife and mother. God never intended for a woman to resent her duties or position in the home. What happens so often in my life is that because I decide I need to be more industrious, I get very busy doing great things for my family, church, and neighbors; but my problems begin when I forget about working on the self-discipline and organization that are important to saving time and energy. Or, I get so busy that I fail to spend time with God and deprive myself of His joy. A virtuous woman is a package deal, if I may use that expression.

We cannot become virtuous without God. Psalm 18:32, 39 say, "It is God that girdeth me with strength, and maketh my way perfect . . . For thou hast girded me with strength unto the battle: thou hast subdued under me those that rose up against me."

The word *strength* in these verses is the same word as *virtuous* in Proverbs 31:10. God binds us with virtue for the battle ahead. I find guarding my home to be very similar to the dangers soldiers face on the battlefield. From snipers (dangers I do not readily see), to front-line attacks (dangers I face daily), to spies (dangers that sneak in to destroy), to lack of courage (the danger of letting up or quitting), I face the enemy constantly. For a mother to say she does not battle threats to her home means that she may be her family's worst enemy, because she has failed to recognize and defend against the dangers that attack her family.

David knew from experience that only God could rescue him from his enemies. Only God could strengthen him for battle. Only God could be his ultimate and absolute Savior. For David to get to this point, He had to believe in God's ability to defend, protect, and save. David testified in Psalm 18:1-2 that God was his strength, his rock, his fortress, his deliverer, his God, his buckler, the horn of his salvation, and his high tower. When we firmly believe that God is all of these things and that He is more than enough to fight our battles, we can stand with David and say that we will trust our God (Psalm 18:1-3). "Give us help from trouble: for vain is the help of man. Through God we shall do valiantly: for he it is that shall tread down our enemies" (Psalm 60:11-12).

The word *valiantly* is the same word as *virtuous* from Proverbs 31:10. Becoming virtuous can only be done through God. We can easily apply these verses to the ever growing popularity of self-help books and magazines. We do not become virtuous by reading more. We do not become virtuous by following man-defined success stories. We do not become virtuous by creating "to do" lists. All of man's ideas about how to become virtuous are vain when God is left out of the equation. Only through God can we be valiant! Why? Because in the midst of the battle, God defeats the enemy. I don't. I can't. I would be the first to quit. But I can with confidence face the enemy, knowing that God will defeat the enemy.

Because God treasures a virtuous woman, I must do all I can to value *becoming* a virtuous woman and to value the virtuous women that surround me. I have no doubt that many of us know of at least one virtuous woman we can do better at treasuring. According to Proverbs 31:10, both finding and being a virtuous woman are rare.

I know my mom is a rare gem. I feel blessed to be able to call her Mom and learn from her for so many years. At the same time, I also have a responsibility to take what I have learned and apply Proverbs 31 to my life. I can better treasure my mom by treasuring what makes her a rare gem. I need to become virtuous. I need to possess the inner strength that grows as I am stretched.

THE WORTH OF THIS TREASURE

Proverbs 31:10

Who can find a virtuous woman? for her price is far above rubies.

- Its Origin: From God
- Its Purpose: To help a woman be a better keeper of her home
- Its Potential: A happy family; a trusting husband

What keeps me from valuing virtue and the virtuous woman? Trying to be virtuous on my own (pride; self-ambition); not recognizing that God values a virtuous woman.

The Trials of Our Faith 3

1 Peter 1:6-7

Wherein ye greatly rejoice, though now for a season, if need be, ye are in heaviness through manifold temptations: That the trial of your faith, being much more precious than of gold that perisheth, though it be tried with fire, might be found unto praise and honour and glory at the appearing of Jesus Christ.

As a pre-teen in the 80s, I grew up watching the Incredible Hulk. My brothers and I would play scenarios from the show, and we would take turns being the Hulk. I don't know why I enjoyed running around, pretending I was mad at everyone. When I look back on those play days, I laugh because the Hulk was really a green man having a temper tantrum. The whole premise of the show was that a doctor could not find a way to control his temper. If he could just control his temper, he would not become a mad, little green man. I don't know of any television shows these days with this premise, but I do know that the concept hits too close to home in today's "angry society."

A friend of mine conducted a survey among schools and found that the number one discipline problem in those schools was anger. The statistic normally would not have startled me except that this survey was conducted among *Christian* schools. Then I began pondering what the home life must be like for these children, because most often angry parents produce angry children. The vicious cycle can be stopped, but nonetheless, the cycle continues more often than not. Even in Christian circles, we are finding little green monsters walking our school halls and sitting in our church pews.

The emotion of anger is not some hopeless disease that victimizes our families. Medications are not the answer to solving temper tantrums. Most often, the emotion of anger is a sinful response to something that displeases us. When we are hurt, discouraged, frustrated, confused, or scared, we often respond to these situations with anger. At the root of our anger is unbelief. We do not believe that God's promises and attributes outlined in the Bible are really effective for our lives. In his study *Taking Time to Quiet Your Soul*, Jim Berg writes, "Unbelief fails to see God as the central component in the picture. It focuses on what displeases *us* instead of what displeases *God*."[1] If unbelief is at the root of anger, then belief becomes the solution to sinful, angry responses.

When Life Falls Apart

Responding to life's many events can be like a roller coaster. We have those thrilling moments: when we lose our first tooth, ride a two-wheel bike for the first time, head off to kindergarten, become a junior higher, graduate from high school, go on our first date, leave home for dorm life, find our true love, choose a career, walk down the wedding aisle, buy a home, discover we are expecting a child, hold our baby for the first time, and the thrills continue. With those thrills also comes heartache on all different levels: scraped knees, bullies, braces, acne, no dates, poor grades despite efforts, shady roommates, deaths of loved ones, debt, poor health, temptations, barren womb, and so many more that knock on our life's door.

How do we respond to these heartaches and trials? Do we become little green men when the rollercoaster begins a descent, and we believe that God has dealt us a crushing blow? Can we read 1 Peter 1:7 and really believe that trials are precious treasures in our lives? According to the Bible, trials—those hard times in our lives when our faith is tested—are more precious than gold.

> 1 Peter 1:6-7—Wherein ye greatly rejoice, though now for a season, if need be, ye are in heaviness through manifold temptations: That the trial of your faith, being much more precious than of gold that perisheth, though it be tried with fire, might be found unto praise and honour and glory at the appearing of Jesus Christ.

Can a scraped knee be a trial of my faith? Yes! Can a mean child in school be a trial of my faith? Yes! Can grief over a lost pet be a trial of my faith? Yes! No matter how minor or major the trial is, and no matter how old or how young a Christian we may be, every moment we hurt, struggle, get frustrated, become confused, are tempted, or are scared is a trial of our faith. It becomes an opportunity for us to draw closer to God, to see Him fulfill His promises, and to trust Him more.

Life does not fall apart for Christians. At times, our poor choices cause some unraveling, making the mending process even more painful; but "life" is not to blame. We often view natural disasters as "life giving us a setback." Life (what the world may term as mother nature, mother earth, the stars, or our destiny) did not give us any set backs, because if we believe the truths spelled out in God's Word, we realize that God is in control of the bigness of weather, the littleness of sparrows, and the simple and complex details in our lives. But if we do not believe that God is in control, we view our lives—the highs and lows—through a distorted tunnel that dead ends with no hope. Or, if we believe that God is in control but fail to comprehend His goodness, we blame God and become angry with Him. Both responses are wrong. God is lovingly weaving my life together into a beautiful tapestry. The pokes of the needle, the knots, and the snips in the canvas are all part of a masterpiece; but we have to believe that God is the Master Weaver. We get so consumed with what the underside of the tapestry looks like in our lives that we fail to trust God to keep weaving together a beautiful creation.

Some Christians do not know God well enough to lean on biblical knowledge and beliefs during hard times. In their book *Values and Virtues*, Howard Hendricks and Bob Phillips quote William Inge: "If we spend sixteen hours a day dealing with tangible things and only five minutes a day dealing with God, is it any wonder that tangible things are two hundred times more real to us than God?"[2] How true! How sad. We do not need to settle for this lifestyle. The more we get to know God, the more we learn that He can be trusted.

Why God Can Be Trusted

God never makes a mistake.
Psalm 18:30—As for God, his way is perfect: the word of the LORD is tried: he is a buckler to all those that trust in him.

Job 34:10-12—Therefore hearken unto me, ye men of understanding: far be it from God, that he should do wickedness; and from the Almighty, that he should commit iniquity. For the work of a man shall he render unto him, and cause every man to find according to his ways. Yea, surely God will not do wickedly, neither will the Almighty pervert judgment.

Psalm 33:4-5—For the word of the Lord is right; and all his works are done in truth. He loveth righteousness and judgment: the earth is full of the goodness of the Lord.

Deuteronomy 32:4—He is the Rock, his work is perfect: for all his ways are judgment: a God of truth and without iniquity, just and right is he.

Psalm 92:15—To shew that the Lord is upright: he is my rock, and there is no unrighteousness in him.

Psalm 145:17—The Lord is righteous in all his ways, and holy in all his works.

Matthew 5:48—Be ye therefore perfect, even as your Father which is in heaven is perfect.

James 1:17—Every good gift and every perfect gift is from above, and cometh down from the Father of lights, with whom is no variableness, neither shadow of turning.

God is always good.

Psalm 68:19—Blessed be the Lord, who daily loadeth us with benefits, even the God of our salvation. Selah.

Exodus 34:6-7—And the Lord passed by before him, and proclaimed, The Lord, The Lord God, merciful and gracious, longsuffering, and abundant in goodness and truth, Keeping mercy for thousands, forgiving iniquity and transgression and sin, and that will by no means clear the guilty; visiting the iniquity of the fathers upon the children, and upon the children's children, unto the third and to the fourth generation.

1 Chronicles 16:34—O give thanks unto the Lord; for he is good; for his mercy endureth for ever.

Psalm 25:8—Good and upright is the Lord: therefore will he teach sinners in the way.

Psalm 33:5—He loveth righteousness and judgment: the earth is full of the goodness of the LORD.

Psalm 34:8—O taste and see that the LORD is good: blessed is the man that trusteth in him.

Psalm 135:3—Praise the LORD; for the LORD is good: sing praises unto his name; for it is pleasant.

Matthew 7:11—If ye then, being evil, know how to give good gifts unto your children, how much more shall your Father which is in heaven give good things to them that ask him?

Lamentations 3:25—The LORD is good unto them that wait for him, to the soul that seeketh him.

Jeremiah 9:23-24—Thus saith the LORD, Let not the wise man glory in his wisdom, neither let the mighty man glory in his might, let not the rich man glory in his riches: But let him that glorieth glory in this, that he understandeth and knoweth me, that I am the LORD which exercise lovingkindness, judgment, and righteousness, in the earth: for in these things I delight, saith the LORD.

Romans 2:4—Or despisest thou the riches of his goodness and forbearance and longsuffering; not knowing that the goodness of God leadeth thee to repentance?

Nahum 1:7—The LORD is good, a strong hold in the day of trouble; and he knoweth them that trust in him.

2 Thessalonians 1:11-12—Wherefore also we pray always for you, that our God would count you worthy of this calling, and fulfil all the good pleasure of his goodness, and the work of faith with power: That the name of our Lord Jesus Christ may be glorified in you, and ye in him, according to the grace of our God and the Lord Jesus Christ.

Psalm 84:11—For the LORD God is a sun and shield: the LORD will give grace and glory: no good thing will he withhold from them that walk uprightly.

God loves me and is for me.

Psalm 56:9—When I cry unto thee, then shall mine enemies turn back: this I know; for God is for me.

Jeremiah 29:11—For I know the thoughts that I think toward you, saith the LORD, thoughts of peace, and not of evil, to give you an expected end.

Matthew 11:28-30—Come unto me, all ye that labour and are heavy laden, and I will give you rest. Take my yoke upon you, and learn of me; for I am meek and lowly in heart: and ye shall find rest unto your souls. For my yoke is easy, and my burden is light.

Romans 8:31-39—What shall we then say to these things? If God be for us, who can be against us? He that spared not his own Son, but delivered him up for us all, how shall he not with him also freely give us all things? Who shall lay any thing to the charge of God's elect? It is God that justifieth. Who is he that condemneth? It is Christ that died, yea rather, that is risen again, who is even at the right hand of God, who also maketh intercession for us. Who shall separate us from the love of Christ? shall tribulation, or distress, or persecution, or famine, or nakedness, or peril, or sword? As it is written, For thy sake we are killed all the day long; we are accounted as sheep for the slaughter. Nay, in all these things we are more than conquerors through him that loved us. For I am persuaded, that neither death, nor life, nor angels, nor principalities, nor powers, nor things present, nor things to come, Nor height, nor depth, nor any other creature, shall be able to separate us from the love of God, which is in Christ Jesus our Lord.

Psalm 139:5-6, 17-18—Thou hast beset me behind and before, and laid thine hand upon me. Such knowledge is too wonderful for me; it is high, I cannot attain unto it. How precious also are thy thoughts unto me, O

God! how great is the sum of them! If I should count them, they are more in number than the sand: when I awake, I am still with thee.

Realizing That Trials Are a Treasure

I have not always viewed trials as positive things in my life. I fought against them for a long time and resented the people responsible for some of them. I did not focus on God during the trials. I thought He cared; but because I did not see Him taking away my problems, I began to doubt His care.

Then I discovered that God was not in the business of taking away my trials! Confused by this Bible principle and hurting from yet another disappointment in my life, I began to study the book of James. What I found in those verses changed my outlook on trials and on God.

I can be joyful in the midst of *all* my trials because they are stepping stones to maturity.

James 1:2-4—My brethren, count it all joy when ye fall into divers temptations; Knowing this, that the trying of your faith worketh patience. But let patience have her perfect work, that ye may be perfect and entire, wanting nothing.

When I falter in my understanding of God or when I get impatient, I must ask Him for wisdom.

James 1:5—If any of you lack wisdom, let him ask of God, that giveth to all men liberally, and upbraideth not; and it shall be given him.

Janie B. Cheaney compares her prayer life and walking by faith to that of a spider building and moving along on its web.

[The prayer] didn't seem like much—just the ability to keep believing enough to ask—but in the end, those prayers were everything. I have seen my own prayers answered in ways and at times I never expected. My faith began as a tremulous thing, a wafting thread that sometimes broke, sometimes wavered. But the years have furnished those anchor points, those times when the Lord graciously invited my testing and even more graciously proved true and firm. Enough that my faith has become less mine and more His—and all the more reliable for that, of

course. After all this time, through all these perplexing troubles, the web became denser, stronger, more beautiful. And, to the world, invisible. [3]

I must believe that God will keep His promises. My belief then gives me stability.

James 1:6-8—But let him ask in faith, nothing wavering. For he that wavereth is like a wave of the sea driven with the wind and tossed. For let not that man think that he shall receive any thing of the Lord. A double minded man is unstable in all his ways.

Trials are not designed to be easy, but the enduring is worth the reward.

James 1:12—Blessed is the man that endureth temptation: for when he is tried, he shall receive the crown of life, which the Lord hath promised to them that love him.

What God allows to happen in my life is a good thing for me.

James 1:17—Every good gift and every perfect gift is from above, and cometh down from the Father of lights, with whom is no variableness, neither shadow of turning.

Because God controls the trials in my life, because they are designed to draw me to Him in maturity, and because I can, by faith, see them as good, I do not need to respond in anger.

James 1:19-21—Wherefore, my beloved brethren, let every man be swift to hear, slow to speak, slow to wrath: For the wrath of man worketh not the righteousness of God. Wherefore lay apart all filthiness and superfluity of naughtiness, and receive with meekness the engrafted word, which is able to save your souls.

I respond correctly by receiving and doing the Word so that I can learn from the trial and grow closer to God because of the trial.

James 1:22-25—But be ye doers of the word, and not hearers only, deceiving your own selves. For if any be a hearer of the word, and not a doer, he is like unto a man beholding his natural face in a glass: For he beholdeth himself, and goeth his way, and straightway forgetteth what manner of man he was. But whoso looketh into the perfect law of liberty, and continueth therein, he being not a forgetful hearer, but a doer of the work, this man shall be blessed in his deed.

After studying James 1 and the chapters that followed, I realized why God saw trials as precious treasures. A trial, designed to bring a Christian closer to God, is a valuable tool that God uses in our lives. In my newfound knowledge of God, I viewed God not as some mean Overseer in heaven spewing out judgments on His people. I saw Him as a loving parent, my heavenly Father, making adjustments in my life—some big, some small, some caused by loved ones, some by strangers, some by natural causes, some by consequences to my poor choices—to draw me closer to Him, to help restore broken fellowship. To me, God no longer was an unfair Judge; He now was a loving Dad.

Valuing the Treasure

This concept of valuing trials might seem strange or confusing: if we are to treasure the very things God treasures, then does this mean that we are to hold in high esteem the very things that hurt us? Yes. But I do not believe the Lord is asking us to go from hospital room to hospital room thanking God for pain, for diseases, or for hurricanes. God is not telling us that we should beg for trials in our lives; He just tells us that they will be a part of our lives, controlled by His goodness and wisdom. If we reminded every grieving person at a funeral that we should be thankful and stop our crying because this loss is a valuable treasure, we would be being insensitive. I do not believe that God is telling us to treasure trials to the degree that we smile through a loved one's funeral or laugh at a broken leg or celebrate when we or someone else is diagnosed with cancer.

My valuing a trial does not make my trial less painful. For instance, the grief over losing a loved one is not less painful because I treasure trials. The wounds of a backstabbing friend do not feel less penetrating because I value trials. The treatments for cancer do not make me less ill because I value trials. It is okay to cry over a painful trial. Tears do not indicate a lack of joy or a disbelief in God's love and providence any more than a smile indicates a presence of happiness and contentment. Even David, a man after God's own heart, had events come into his life that made him cry unto God.

In valuing trials, what should my response be to others who go through a trial? Do I have a responsibility as a brother or sister in Christ to value another's trial? When Paul writes in Galatians 6:2 for us to "bear ye one another's burden," I believe he is exhorting us to value another's trial knowing that the trial is present in one's life with God's permission. Praying for and being compassionate for children with scraped knees and bloody noses, barren women, grieving church members, and hurting parents are all part of bearing one another's burdens—valuing the trials of others.

We value a trial by giving God the glory.

In his first epistle, Peter tells his readers to not consider a trial as unusual in a Christian's life. He even calls the trial a *fiery* one, able to ignite and smelter, which implies that some trials that we face are going to be hard to endure. But Peter also tells his readers to rejoice to the point that they can be a part of Christ's sufferings as the gospel is spread abroad. He concludes by saying that a trial is an indication that the Spirit of God resides in a Christian.

> 1 Peter 4:12-14, 16—Beloved, think it not strange concerning the fiery trial which is to try you, as though some strange thing happened unto you: But rejoice, inasmuch as ye are partakers of Christ's sufferings; that, when his glory shall be revealed, ye may be glad also with exceeding joy. If ye be reproached for the name of Christ, happy are ye; for the spirit of glory and of God resteth upon you: on their part he is evil spoken of, but on your part he is glorified . . . Yet if any man suffer as a Christian, let him not be ashamed; but let him glorify God on this behalf.

We value a trial by believing and living the truth of God's faithfulness.

Psalm 84:11 promises that "no good thing will He withhold" from us if we walk uprightly. Romans 8:28 promises that "all things work together for good" for us when we love God. [4] If we face a trial and doubt God's faithfulness, that trial will not work in our lives the way God intended for it to work. If we face a trial and doubt God's faithfulness, our response will be anger and resentment. We cannot afford to doubt God's faithfulness!

> 1 Peter 4:19—Wherefore let them that suffer according to the will of God commit the keeping of their souls to him in well doing, as unto **a** faithful Creator.

1 Corinthians 10:13—There hath no temptation taken you but such as is common to man: but God is faithful, who will not suffer you to be tempted above that ye are able; but will with the temptation also make a way to escape, that ye may be able to bear it.

Deuteronomy 31:6—Be strong and of a good courage, fear not, nor be afraid of them: for the LORD thy God, he it is that doth go with thee; he will not fail thee, nor forsake thee.

Psalm 37:28—For the LORD loveth judgment, and forsaketh not his saints; they are preserved for ever: but the seed of the wicked shall be cut off.

Psalm 94:14—For the LORD will not cast off his people, neither will he forsake his inheritance.

Lamentations 3:22-24—It is of the LORD's mercies that we are not consumed, because his compassions fail not. They are new every morning: great is thy faithfulness. The LORD is my portion, saith my soul; therefore will I hope in him.

Hebrews 10:22-23—Let us draw near with a true heart in full assurance of faith, having our hearts sprinkled from an evil conscience, and our bodies washed with pure water. Let us hold fast the profession of our faith without wavering; (for he is faithful that promised;)

1 John 1:9—If we confess our sins, he is faithful and just to forgive us our sins, and to cleanse us from all unrighteousness.

We value trials by drawing near to God as a result of experiencing the trial.
When we see the trial for what it is—a stepping stone in our relationship with Christ—we value it for the very same reason that God values it. We are never commanded in Scripture to enjoy trials; we are commanded to endure them and count them as an opportunity to give God glory.

Recently, I heard a preacher say that God used trials in David's life to keep a tight leash on David so that he would not stray. The more I attempt to live a God-honoring Christian life, the more I believe that I need leashes in my life, too, to keep me closer to God. I can say this confidently because I firmly believe that God will only give me what I can handle as I depend on Him. God can be trusted because He never makes a mistake, because He is always good, and because He loves me and is for me.

In our Christian life, we will never get to the point of treasuring trials until we firmly believe that God is enough to sustain and preserve us through a trial for His glory. Through both good times and hard times, we have to be willing to say, "To God be the glory, great things He hath done."[5]

FORMULA FOR TREASURING TRIALS

God never makes a mistake

God is always good

God loves me and is for me

- I can trust in the midst of a trial
- God gives hope and comfort in the midst of a trial
- I can enjoy sweeter fellowship with God as a result of the trial
- As I communicate my trust in Him, I will glorify Him

THE WORTH OF THIS TREASURE

1 Peter 1:6-7

Wherein ye greatly rejoice, though now for a season, if need be, ye are in heaviness through manifold temptations: That the trial of your faith, being much more precious than of gold that perisheth, though it be tried with fire, might be found unto praise and honour and glory at the appearing of Jesus Christ.

- Its Origin: From God
- Its Purpose: To help draw one closer to God; to be purified
- Its Potential: A sweeter relationship with God for His glory

What keeps me from valuing the trials of my faith? My sinful responses; my lack of trust; my unbelief.

Marriage 4

Hebrews 13:4

Marriage is honourable in all, and the bed undefiled: but whoremongers and adulterers God will judge.

I love being married. Having been surrounded by many good marriages, I have seen firsthand how a biblical love can transform and unite a couple for God's glory. The divorce statistics in America are alarming, and the rate of failure for Christian marriages is no different than the rate of failure for non-Christian couples. Obviously, many couples—Christian and non-Christian—possess a treasure but are failing to value the treasure.

I am no expert in marriage counseling, but I can look back in my own marriage and see that the hard times happened more because I failed to value my marriage and my man than because of any other problems. When we find a spouse and say, "I do," we take possession of a valuable treasure called marriage. The word *honourable* in Hebrews 13:4 is the same word as *precious* that we already studied from 1 Peter 1:7 where Peter writes that our trials are precious in God's sight. Marriage is precious; it is a treasure. Divorce or unhappy marriages occur when one or both spouses fail to value that treasure. Learning to value what God values results in strong and productive marriages.

Treasure Robbers

Anytime something is deemed valuable, the threat of it being stolen becomes greater. If marriage were not valuable, it would not be worth defending. Because God declares my marriage precious, every day of my marriage, I must defend against attacks that threaten it.

Satan knows that if he destroys a marriage, he has then marred the picture of Christ and His church (Ephesians 5:23-27). I am humbled when I ponder the truth that our marriages should reflect to our children Christ's sacrificial love and servant leadership. I am inadequate to do that task by myself, but God clearly intended marriage to mirror Christ's relationship to the church. In our home, my husband Steve and I become ambassadors of the gospel to the watchful eyes of our children, unsaved neighbors, or co-workers. In this gospel context, I begin to better understand why God considers our marriage precious to Him. The question I must answer every day is whether or not I properly represent the church's ideal relationship with Christ to my children through the way I interact, respond, and love my husband. It is no wonder that Satan wants to work diligently to destroy my marriage.

As the ultimate treasure robber, Satan spews out many lies that are brightly wrapped in appealing paper, making the devil's gift appealing but truly a ticking bomb. I say "ticking bomb" because Satan destroys a marriage in subtle ways. Inside his prettily wrapped gift box are lies that seem sensible but are far from truthful. Compare these conversations to Satan's conversation with Eve in Genesis 3.

"Did God say, 'Thou shalt not commit adultery'?" asks Satan.

"Yes," I respond. "He said that a man and woman shall be one and that adultery is forbidden."

Satan laughs, "Adultery is not forbidden. It is natural, and God knows that and will understand your desire to be with more than one person. Besides, He'll forgive you anyway."

"Did God say, 'Pride comes before destruction'?" asks Satan.

"Yes," I respond. "He said that by humility we can be exalted and that we should think of others more than ourselves."

Satan laughs, "Then who's going to look after you? When you love yourself more fully, you will be able to love others better."

"Did God say, 'Fornication is a sin'?" asks Satan.

"Yes," I respond. "He said that fornication is a sin against the body and that we were created for God and not for sexual gratification."

Satan laughs, "If God created sexual pleasures, then why is it wrong to receive that gratification, no matter where it comes from? Pleasing one's self is natural and therefore okay."

"Did God say, 'Submit yourselves to your husbands'?" asks Satan.

"Yes," I respond. "Just as Christ is the head of the church, God says that the man is the head of the home and that I should submit to my husband's leadership."

Satan laughs, "Don't you recall that God created the woman because the man couldn't do it on his own? God didn't expect you to be under a man but to be equal to him in all things. You owe it to yourself to be someone in the home. You're not the maid!"

Over and over again, Satan finds ways to twist the truth to deceive us. Following common sense or what seems natural to us is a humanistic, relativistic way of approaching life. In essence, we leave our Creator out of our decision making. When a created being chooses to defy its Creator, the creation is in a state of rebellion. Satan succeeds in robbing us—by getting us to undermine our marriage commitment—when he succeeds in getting us to disagree with God. Eve heard both the truth from her Creator and Satan's ticking bomb of reasoning, and then chose to disagree with her Creator and agree with Satan. Shortly afterward, Eve discovered that her Creator was right and her Deceiver was wrong. Truth does not have to make sense to be truth; God's ways do not have to make sense to be right. God is truth, and He is right . . . always. God's Word verifies this right path.

Isaiah 55:8-9—For my thoughts are not your thoughts, neither are your ways my ways, saith the LORD. For as the heavens are higher than the earth, so are **my ways** higher than your ways, and my thoughts than your thoughts.

Psalm 95:10—Forty years long was I grieved with this generation, and said, It is a people that do err in their heart, and they have not known **my ways**.

Ezekiel 18:29-31—Yet saith the house of Israel, **The way of the Lord** is not equal. O house of Israel, are not my ways equal? are not your ways unequal? Therefore I will judge you, O house of Israel, every one according to his ways, saith the LORD GOD. Repent, and turn yourselves from all your transgressions; so iniquity shall not be your ruin. Cast away from you all your transgressions, whereby ye have transgressed; and make you a new heart and a new spirit: for why will ye die, O house of Israel?

Proverbs 10:29—The **way of the LORD** is strength to the upright: but destruction shall be to the workers of iniquity.

John 14:6—Jesus saith unto him, **I am the way**, the truth, and the life: no man cometh unto the Father, but by me.

We are our own worst enemy when we allow our marital treasure to be robbed and destroyed. When we do not believe God, we err in our hearts. "Take heed, brethren, lest there be in any of you an evil heart of unbelief, in departing from the living God. But exhort one another daily, while it is called Today; lest any of you be hardened through the deceitfulness of sin" (Hebrews 3:12-13).

Must-believe Truths

Hebrews 3:12 calls an unbelieving heart an evil heart that has departed from God. If I treasure my marriage by protecting it against Satan and his thieves, I must secure my home with basic, uncompromising beliefs about God and marriage. Failing to believe these truths is like failing to put locks and alarm systems in my home. These are "must-believe" truths that will fortify our hearts and minds against Satan's lies and keep our marriages strong.

I must believe that God is holy and that I am in need of His holiness.

- Isaiah 57:15—For thus saith the high and lofty One that inhabiteth eternity, whose name is **Holy**; I dwell in the high and holy place, with him also that is of a contrite and humble spirit, to revive the spirit of the humble, and to revive the heart of the contrite ones.
- 1 Samuel 2:2-3—There is none **holy** as the LORD: for there is none beside thee: neither is there any rock like our God. Talk no more so exceeding proudly; let not arrogancy come out of your mouth: for the LORD is a God of knowledge, and by him actions are weighed.

I must believe that God is love and that I am in need of His love.

- Jeremiah 31:3—The LORD hath appeared of old unto me, saying, Yea, I have loved thee with an **everlasting love**: therefore with lovingkindness have I drawn thee.
- Ephesians 2:4-5—But God, who is rich in mercy, for his **great love** wherewith he loved us, Even when we were dead in sins, hath quickened us together with Christ, (by grace ye are saved).

I must believe that God is right and that I am in need of His righteousness and instruction in righteousness.

- Ezra 9:15—O LORD God of Israel, thou art **righteous**: for we remain yet escaped, as it is this day: behold, we are before thee in our trespasses: for we cannot stand before thee because of this.
- Hosea 14:9—Who is wise, and he shall understand these things? prudent, and he shall know them? for the ways of the LORD are **right**, and the just shall walk in them: but the transgressors shall fall therein.
- 2 Timothy 3:16-17—All scripture is given by inspiration of God, and is profitable for doctrine, for reproof, for correction, for **instruction in righteousness**: That the man of God may be perfect, throughly furnished unto all good works.

I must believe that God is just and that I am in need of His mercy.

- Micah 7:9—I will bear the indignation of the LORD, because I have sinned against him, until he plead my cause, and **execute judgment** for me: he will bring me forth to the light, and I shall behold his righteousness.
- Ecclesiastes 12:14—For God shall bring **every work into judgment**, with every secret thing, whether it be good, or whether it be evil.

I must believe that God is powerful and that I am in need of His protection.

- Ephesians 1:19-20—And what is the exceeding greatness of his **power** to us-ward who believe, according to the working of his mighty power, Which he wrought in Christ, when he raised him from the dead, and set him at his own right hand in the heavenly places,

- Matthew 19:24-26—And again I say unto you, It is easier for a camel to go through the eye of a needle, than for a rich man to enter into the kingdom of God. When his disciples heard it, they were exceedingly amazed, saying, Who then can be saved? But Jesus beheld them, and said unto them, With men this is impossible; but **with God all things are possible.**

I must believe that God is kind and that I am in need of His care.
- Titus 3:4-7—But after that the **kindness** and love of God our Saviour toward man appeared, Not by works of righteousness which we have done, but according to his mercy he saved us, by the washing of regeneration, and renewing of the Holy Ghost; Which he shed on us abundantly through Jesus Christ our Saviour; That being justified by his grace, we should be made heirs according to the hope of eternal life.
- Psalm 36:7-8—How excellent is thy **lovingkindness**, O God! therefore the children of men put their trust under the shadow of thy wings. They shall be abundantly satisfied with the fatness of thy house; and thou shalt make them drink of the river of thy pleasures.
- 1 Peter 5:7—Casting all your care upon him; for he **careth** for you.

I must believe that God is for me and that I am in need of His grace.
- Psalm 86:5—For thou, Lord, art **good**, and ready to forgive; and plenteous in mercy unto all them that call upon thee.
- Nahum 1:7—The LORD is **good**, a strong hold in the day of trouble; and he knoweth them that trust in him.
- Psalm 139:17-18—How precious also are thy thoughts unto me, O God! how great is the sum of them! If I should count them, they are more in number than the sand: when I awake, **I am still with thee**.

I must believe that God is faithful and that I can trust Him.
- Lamentations 3:22-23—It is of the LORD's mercies that we are not consumed, because his compassions fail not. They are new every morning: great is thy **faithfulness**.
- Deuteronomy 7:8-10—But because the LORD loved you, and because he would keep the oath which he had sworn unto your fathers, hath

the LORD brought you out with a mighty hand, and redeemed you out of the house of bondmen, from the hand of Pharaoh king of Egypt. Know therefore that the LORD thy God, he is God, the **faithful** God, which keepeth covenant and mercy with them that love him and keep his commandments to a thousand generations; And repayeth them that hate him to their face, to destroy them: he will not be slack to him that hateth him, he will repay him to his face.

- 1 Corinthians 10:13—There hath no temptation taken you but such as is common to man: but God is **faithful**, who will not suffer you to be tempted above that ye are able; but will with the temptation also make a way to escape, that ye may be able to bear it.

Must-believe Truths

God's holiness exposes my sin. My sin separates me from God and sends me to hell. God's love outlines a rescue plan through His Son Jesus Christ. When I believe in Jesus' death and resurrection as my Propitiator and confess my sins to God, I experience God's righteous deliverance from an eternal death in hell. God's justice demanded blameless blood to be shed for my justification. His mercy provided a Lamb when I deserved the cross. As His child, I now have full and bold access to God's power, which includes His Spirit and His strength to overcome my deepest fears and sinful struggles, as well as His protective arms to shield me from the satanic darts that I cannot handle. On a daily basis, I feel God's kindness toward me as He cares for my every need and even extends blessings beyond my hopes and expectations. He does all of this because He is for me. He is my Father, my God, my Creator. And because I am His child, He graciously continues to give to me what I do not deserve, including forgiveness of sin, as I remember all that He has done for me and humbly acknowledge that He is the God of holiness, love, righteousness, justice, power, and kindness. Contrary to what my sinful nature tells me, I am inadequate to be or do anything without God. Yet, God, Who is the same yesterday, today, and forever, faithfully fulfills His every promise to me. Therefore, I can and must trust Him for everything He places and performs in my life. This trust and obedience to God brings me joy unspeakable and compels me to worship Him for Who He is and how He has saved me.

When I fail to believe these basic truths, I begin to leave my marriage vulnerable to robbers. Faith in these *must-believe truths* is like putting locks on my treasure box of marriage. By fortifying my heart and my mind with these truths, I stabilize and fireproof my marriage against Satan's attacks and fiery darts. When Satan attacks, he aims for my belief system (my faith), causing my thoughts and eventually my actions to fall to his deceitful ways.

When I am firmly established in these *must-believe truths,* I represent the gospel more clearly and more effectively to my family, neighbors, co-workers, friends, community, and church family. I not only stabilize my marriage but also my relationship with Christ and others by believing these basic truths from God's treasure map, the Bible.

Where we most often fail in these *must-believe truths* is *not* that we do not believe that God is holy, right, merciful, and gracious, but that we fail in believing that *we need* God's holiness, righteousness, mercy, and grace. When pride rears its ugly head in my life, I am failing to believe that I need God. In marriage, when one or both spouses believe they can live the Christian life without God and His help, they are exposing themselves and their marriage to thieves who desire to destroy their treasure and make it useless for God.

These truths need to be rehearsed in our minds over and over again. They should be memorized so that we can effectively meditate on them. The stronger my faith becomes, the more fortified my life is against the dangers of this world. This faith must be grounded in God's truth, not in what makes sense to mankind. I have put a copy-and-cut page in Appendix C to aid readers in rehearsing these basic truths.

Treasuring My Marriage

Once we understand why God treasures the union of marriage and once we have installed the necessary locks and alarm systems in our marriage, how can we best treasure the uniting of one man to one woman? Because I am not the expert on this matter, and because I am still learning how to treasure my marriage, I will share the tidbits (*truthbits*) that my grandparents and parents have passed on to Steve and me either by word or example.

Before I got married, my parents presented me with a booklet that they had written together—a compilation of some sound wisdom for me to adhere to so that my marriage would be strong. From time to time (but not often enough), I open my cloth-bound book of sound marriage advice and review its contents. The first page of the book is a letter to me from my dad:

> *Dear Shannon,*
>
> *Your mother and I love you and cherish the thoughts of your childhood. We now look forward in great anticipation to your future with Steve. The Lord has truly been good to us and to you.*
>
> *I am enclosing some thoughts and "tried and true" suggestions for your future. Most probably they are not new to you, but some of us Brocks need to get our thoughts down on paper.*
>
> *God is always faithful; trust Him.*
>
> *Your dad,*
> *DAD*
> *July 30, 1993*

Out of all of the words my dad wrote in that letter, the ones that really inspire me emotionally, energize me mentally, and resonate with me spiritually are "God is always faithful; trust Him." Oh how I have needed to hear those words during some difficult humps in my life. Even though I was moving away from my dad's day-to-day care, I could still picture my dad bending over and whispering in my ear, "God is always faithful; trust Him."

After the letter came just a few pages of *truthbits* that I could not afford to ignore. My parents wrote,

1. Growth intellectually, in physical abilities, in relationship skills, and in spiritual understanding are good, desirable, important, essential, and are *your* personal responsibility, *your* decision, and *your* effort; yet you can only grow through the grace of God.
2. Find the wise people and go to them for advice. A wise person is not always the smart, experienced, opinionated, expressive, pushy, slow-to-decide, supportive person in your life. When you do find those who are truly wise, listen carefully.

3. Seasons will come and seasons will go. God gives us variety in our life, and we need to be content with the season we are in. Remember, no matter the season, there is hardship there and that is okay. Look for the blessings and joys in that season. (The woods are full of them. Like deer, you sometimes have to hunt for them.) You may never have the opportunity of this season again—ever—so look hard and have fun.

4. Expectations of life, marriage, occupation, and the future are sometimes different from reality. So, always remember "My soul, wait thou only upon God; for my expectation is from Him" (Psalm 62:5).

5. Be content with what your Creator, Savior, and God brings your way, whether they be blessings beyond measure or trials for growth.

Nestled between the pages of spiritual and practical advice, my dad included a few important tips about how I should treat and cherish my husband. He began by stating, "Most hubbies are sensitive, yet sometimes ignorant creatures, and need to be treated correctly." He then wrote that such treatment "insures longevity of relationship, reciprocal treatment, and domestic tranquility." His tips continued.

1. Back scratches are important. They not only feel good, but are also very good in communicating your current state of mind.

2. Touching (without sex) communicates love. Do it often.

3. Speak the truth in love—which means talk it out since men aren't mind readers, talk truthfully, and always speak in a loving and kind spirit.

4. Don't smother your man. What woman is really happy with a man who always asks her permission?

5. Don't be afraid to cry, but don't use tears and/or your happiness as a weapon or tool of manipulation.

6. Challenge your man to take a few risks, to grow, to rise above the ordinary but while you are challenging, don't nag, harp, or whine. Use your head, Girl. He is a man, not a machine. Follow the leader, and he's your leader.

7. Happy, secure, obedient, and well-adjusted children are a natural outcome of a husband and wife who communicate and love each other while loving and obeying the "God of our Fathers."

8. Where you live is never as important as how you live there. Always work at making the house (his and yours) home. There should be "no place like home."

9. Keep studying the man. Your man is complex and it will take some thought and concentration, as well as study and Bible reading to figure him out again and again. Find the Bible formulas; they always work.

10. Never quit. *Can't never did do nothin'!*

11. The best advice I can give you on this subject of caring for your man is to go to your mom for advice; she got it right!

Thanks, Dad, for getting it right, too. Your words and your example were and continue to be a lighthouse in my quest to also get it right. Thank you for reminding and advising me by word and example that "God is always faithful; trust Him." Your lighthouse pointed me to the haven of God's Word.

Treasuring Marriage When I Am Not Married

This chapter is not just for the married person, because learning to treasure what God treasures does not necessarily begin the moment we possess the treasure. One of the best parts of Christmas is the anticipation of the gift we always wanted. Just as I have met few people who do not anticipate Christmas morning, I have met few people in life who do not desire to get married. For most of us, the desire for marriage and companionship is very strong. We anticipate it; we hope for it. But despite one's anticipation, God does not call everyone to be married, nor should a single person consider singleness to be a lesser calling. Paul speaks of his singleness as purposeful and effective.

> 1 Corinthians 7:32-33—But I would have you without carefulness. He that is unmarried careth for the things that belong to the LORD, how he may please the Lord: But he that is married careth for the things that are of the world, how he may please his wife.

How I view marriage and the guidelines set forth in the Bible about marriage *before* I am married says a great deal about how I will treasure my marriage once I am married. I have great respect for single people who go out of their way to respect and honor the marriage relationship.

There are moments in my marriage when I will mention to my husband, "Stay away from that woman." The issue is not whether I trust Steve but that I do *not* trust the woman. The Bible calls certain women *strange* for a reason, and the Bible also tells us to run from these women. Steve appreciates my hints and has learned to be sensitive to my intuition. And the conversation can be vice versa. "Shannon, stay away from that man. He doesn't live within any boundaries." I have learned to listen and follow my husband's discernment. Strange women and fence-less men do not treasure marriage, and we—married or single—need to avoid them.

As parents, Steve and I want to teach our children when they reach their teenage years to honor and treasure marriage, even though they are not married. The following are just a few of our curriculum objectives in teaching them to treasure marriage before they are married.

1. Marriage is a privilege, not a right. Be worthy of a godly spouse if ever God gives you one.

2. Do not covet other people's spouses. They are taken. They belong to someone else. Covetousness is a sin of the heart that eventually shows up in our thoughts and actions. Kill covetousness and dwell on the *must-believe* truths of the Bible.

3. Do not overstay the invitations from married couples. Appreciate their hospitality, but know when to depart. You may be best friends to a married man or woman, but that does not mean you spend every day off or free weekend at their home. Know when your married friends need family time with just family. This may mean you say *no* to an invitation.

4. Never ever joke about the sins of adultery or fornication or make light of sex and the marriage vows. A married couple vows to honor and be faithful to each other. As a Christian brother or sister in Christ, you must commit to honor the marriage union of others in what you say, what you think, what you watch, and what you listen to.

5. Set boundaries in how you react and respond to married couples. Go the extra mile to avoid being accused of flirting. Avoid all appearances of evil. Remember that your heart is deceitful and wicked. Practice biblical love. Refuse to entertain those who dishonor marriage.

6. Watch married couples; learn from them. Develop biblical strategies for making your marriage honorable before the Lord.

7. Remember that men and women (even those who profess to be Christians) can be like the *strange* women mentioned in Proverbs. Run from them and to God. Know and believe what God says about marriage and the marriage union in order to discern when others are *not* treasuring marriage. Avoid those people!

8. Serve the families and couples in your local church. Nurture the couples in your church by supporting them through babysitting, signing up for nursery, volunteering to do children's ministries, financing scholarships to couples' retreats, and encouraging marriage and family conferences. Marriage and the family were instituted by God. Both need nurturing.

9. Be faithful to God first. In James 4 God speaks of spiritual unfaithfulness to Him as adultery. Learn first to be spiritually faithful to God; then you will be prepared to be faithful in your future marriage.

10. God is always enough for you. He is faithful, and you can trust Him.

Valuing What God Values

As a married person, is my marriage an accurate reflection of Christ's relationship to the church? Have I been deceived by Satan's lies? Have I slid away from being grounded in the truths of God's Word? Is my belief system firmly bound to God's truths? Am I leaning on my own understanding? Do I realize that the same *must-believe* truths also relate to my spouse? Have I quit treasuring my marriage, my spouse, my family, my relationship with Christ?

As a single person, do I honor the marriages around me? Do I really believe that God can be trusted? Am I content with God's will in my life? Do I realize that the must-believe truths are foundational, even for a single person?

Marriage is a treasure to God because its union reflects Christ's relationship to the church. It is no wonder that God values marriage, declaring it a precious representation of Christ's sacrifice for the church. What an awesome responsibility to represent the church's relationship to Jesus Christ! What an amazing gift from God!

THE WORTH OF THIS TREASURE

Hebrews 13:4

Marriage is honourable in all, and the bed undefiled: but whoremongers and adulterers God will judge.

- Its Origin: Instituted by God; obtained the minute we say, "I do."
- Its Purpose: To represent the union of Christ and the church
- Its Potential: Companionship; help; children and family that live forever

What keeps me from valuing marriage? My choices; my poor belief system; my listening to and reading secular advice.

God's Promises

2 Peter 1:4

Whereby are given unto us exceeding great and precious promises: that by these ye might be partakers of the divine nature, having escaped the corruption that is in the world through lust.

I cannot imagine the terror that David faced. If Saul was not after him, the Philistines were. Over and over again David had to escape constant danger. His highs and lows had to be exhausting. Psalm 56 records one such incident where David found himself in the hands of his enemy, the Philistines. At a time when David could have easily blamed God for his harrowing situation, he chose to trust God. Verse 9 says, "When I cry unto thee, then shall mine enemies turn back: this I know; for God is for me." The phrase *for God is for me* is an amazing tribute to David's faith. The easy road for David, or for any of us, would be to say that God is for us when we have escaped danger or when we have survived a hard trial; but David said, "God is for me," while he was in the midst of danger.

Charles Spurgeon commentates about the phrase *God is for me.*

It is impossible for any human speech to express the full meaning of this delightful phrase, "God is for me." He was "for us" before the worlds were made; He was "for us," or He would not have given His well-beloved Son; He was "for us" when He smote the Only-begotten, and laid the full weight of His wrath upon Him—He was "for us," though He was against Him; He was "for us," when we were ruined in the fall—He loved us notwithstanding all; He was "for us," when we were rebels against Him, and with a high hand were bidding Him defiance; He was "for us," or He would not have brought us humbly to seek His face. He has been "for us" in many struggles; we have been summoned to encounter hosts of dangers; we have been assailed by temptations from without and within—how could we have remained unharmed to this hour if He had not been "for us"? He is "for us," with all the infinity of His being; with all the omnipotence of His love; with all the infallibility of His wisdom; arrayed in all His divine attributes, He is "for us,"—eternally and

71

immutably "for us"; "for us" when yon blue skies shall be rolled up like a worn out vesture; "for us" throughout eternity. And because He is "for us," the voice of prayer will always ensure His help. [1]

That God is *for me* is an incredible truth that we need to claim and trust, but the assurance of David's "this I know" brings goose bumps to my skin. From a personal relationship with God, from eyewitness accounts and experiences, from stories told of his rich heritage, from a knowledge of God that was learned from the Scriptures, David knew that God was for him. His past—the things he learned and witnessed—supported his faith, but his present situation—the treachery and conspiracy—tempted his faith, yet he trusted God. He knew God was for him. He did not doubt it. He rested in it. David knew beyond a shadow of any doubt that God was for him. The confidence that his believing this truth brought David was tremendous. With confidence David faced a bear and lion; with confidence David faced Goliath; with confidence David faced Saul's hatred; with confidence David faced threats of being stoned; with confidence David faced the unknown; with confidence David turned to God during all of the highs and lows of his life. *This I know; for God is for me.* What a truth-packed motto to live by.

David claimed a promise, and believing the promise changed his life. God has given us promises, and He has called these promises *great* and *precious* (2 Peter 1:4). In other words, He has given us the greatest promises possible, and they are valuable treasures in God's sight. These same promises, precious as they are to God, should be treasures we value in our lives.

Noah Webster wrote, "In Scripture, the promise of God is the declaration or assurance which God has given in his word of bestowing blessings on his people. Such assurance resting on the perfect justice, power, benevolence and immutable veracity of God, cannot fail of performance."[2] Webster spoke of assurance that cannot fail because the object of his assurance rests in a perfect God. Webster's statement reminds me of David's confidence in Psalm 56:9: "This I know; for God is for me." The trouble we encounter so often is that we find ourselves doubting the promises of God. We either do not know the promises, do not believe the promises, or do not consider the promises to be relevant to today; therefore, we fail to claim the promises of God.

"Just how good are these promises?" asks A. W. Tozer. "As good as the character of the One who made them." He goes on to write, "[God] is a holy God who cannot lie, the God who is infinitely rich and who can make good on all His promises! He is the God who is infinitely honest—He has never cheated anyone! He is the God who is infinitely true. Just as good and true as God is—that is how good and true His promises are."[3]

To better illustrate, let us think for a moment. What if someone gave us a painting and told us the painting was worth one million dollars? If we truly believed the painting was worth one million dollars, we would handle the painting much differently than if we believed the painting was a ten-dollar garage-sale special. What we believe about something or someone determines how we treat and/or respond to the thing or person. In the same way, what we truly believe about God and His promises will determine how we treat God and respond to Him and His promises. We will not apply God's promises to our lives if we do not believe those promises are relevant and true for us today.

- If I do not believe that God is enough, I will not live like He is enough.
- If I do not believe that God forgives, I will not live like He forgives.
- If I do not believe that God is with me, I will not live like He is near me.
- If I do not believe that God answers me when I call, I will not live like He hears me.
- If I do not believe that God loves me and takes care of me, I will not live like I am loved.
- If I do not believe that God's promises are treasures in my life, I will not claim those treasures in my life.

"Claiming" Promises

The word *claim* is not in the Bible, but we use it often when we talk about the importance of "claiming God's promises." The earliest record of *claim* being used is in the 14th century and is found in the French and Latin languages. This Latin word *kalare* means "to call, to cry out, to shout." The English word *clamor* comes from this same Latin root word *kalare*. By studying the etymology of *claim*, I found that the word is cross-referenced to an Old English word *hlowan* which means "to make noise like a cow." (Our current word *low* comes from this same Old English word.) This earliest use of *claim* has a boisterous, demanding, almost annoying connotation. [4] All I can picture is an ornery, needing-to-be-milked, never-been-starved cow standing outside the barn bawling and carrying on until the farmer gets tired of listening to the clamor. And when *claim* is used this way when speaking about how a Christian should just "claim God's promises," I picture a demanding, noisily complaining person standing with his fist pointed into the sky expressing disappointment to God for not getting what he wanted. I see little difference in the cow's "moo-moo" and the person's "boo-hoo."

If claiming promises means that we, like the cow, make noise until we are attended to, then we are straying from understanding why God recorded so many promises in His Word. What I really like is the use of the word *claim* that originated in the mid-1800s during the Gold Rush days and was associated with property deeds and insurance terminology. A miner would scope out the land and then enter the assayer's office to check to see if the land was available. If it was, the assayer would record the miner's name as the new owner of the land, and the land became the miner's right and property. The miner would then go to his land and stake his claim by burying landmarks at the corners of his property. God has recorded in Scripture the promises that are available to us. The Almighty Assayer has spoken, and we are now the rightful heirs to great and precious promises. As His children, we can now go out and stake our claim. God has recorded His covenant, and we are the recipients of His covenant (Hebrews 9:15-16). Just as a miner can confidently pound in the stakes marking his new claim, we, too, as God's children can confidently go through life staking our claim to God's promises.

When I do not feel forgiven, I need to stake my claim to 1 John 1:9. "If we confess our sins, he is faithful and just to forgive us our sins, and to cleanse us from all unrighteousness."

When I feel at war with my thoughts, I need to stake my claim to Isaiah 26:3. "Thou wilt keep him in perfect peace, whose mind is stayed on thee: because he trusteth in thee."

When I feel helpless, I need to stake my claim to Job 42:2. "I know that thou canst do every thing, and that no thought can be withholden from thee."

When I feel alone, I need to stake my claim to Psalm 27:10. "When my father and my mother forsake me, then the LORD will take me up."

When it seems my prayers go unheard, I need to stake my claim to Jeremiah 33:3. "Call unto me, and I will answer thee, and shew thee great and mighty things, which thou knowest not."

When I feel lost with no direction, I need to stake my claim to Psalm 23. "The Lord is my Shepherd, I shall not want . . . He leadeth me . . . "

When I do not feel like obeying, I need to stake my claim to John 15:10-11. "If ye keep my commandments, ye shall abide in my love; even as I have kept my Father's commandments, and abide in his love. These things have I spoken unto you, that my joy might remain in you, and that your joy might be full."

When I am tired and weary, I need to stake my claim to Matthew 11:28-30. "Come unto me, all ye that labour and are heavy laden, and I will give you rest. Take my yoke upon you, and learn of me; for I am meek and lowly in heart: and ye shall find rest unto your souls. For my yoke is easy, and my burden is light."

When I get discouraged, I need to stake my claim to John 14:1-3. "Let not your heart be troubled: ye believe in God, believe also in me. In my Father's house are many mansions: if it were not so, I would have told you. I go to prepare a place for you. And if I go and prepare a place for you, I will come again, and receive you unto myself; that where I am, there ye may be also."

When I feel tempted to sin or to doubt, I need to stake my claim to 1 Corinthians 10:12-13. "Wherefore let him that thinketh he standeth take heed lest he fall. There hath no temptation taken you but such as is common to man: but God is faithful, who will not suffer you to be tempted above that ye are able; but will with the temptation also make a way to escape, that ye may be able to bear it."

These promises are my claim. I do not need to make any demands of God. I do not need to make terrible noises so that He will get tired of hearing me and finally give me what I want. These promises are already mine. They are in my possession as a child of God. I own them. But when I fail to believe them or take possession of them, I fail to stake my claim.

My life verse is 2 Timothy 1:12. Paul, under God's inspiration, writes, "For the which cause I also suffer these things: nevertheless I am not ashamed: for I know whom I have believed, and am persuaded that he is able to keep that which I have committed unto him against that day." This verse tells me that *God is for me*. I believe in God. I am convinced that God will keep His promises. He made a commitment to keep me, and He will. I am confident. In other words, I have staked my claim on God and His Word.

Claiming is not making a lot of cow noise. Claiming is believing. Claiming is not complaining. Claiming is believing, which produces a confident expectation of fulfilled promises. Claiming is not demanding. Claiming is trusting God to honor the promises He has already given to us; it is waiting on His timing (Psalm 62:5; Isaiah 40). We can begin to treasure His great and precious promises by staking our claim to them. Believing, confidently expecting, and trusting.

Treasuring Promises
Staking our claim to God's promises is an important first step to treasuring God's promises. The next step to treasuring God's promises is meditating on God and His Word. David wrote in Psalm 63:5-7, "My soul shall be satisfied as with marrow and fatness; and my mouth shall praise thee with joyful lips: When I remember thee upon my bed, and meditate on thee in the night watches. Because thou hast been my help, therefore in the shadow of thy wings will I rejoice."

Psalm 63 has been called a wilderness psalm because David wrote this Psalm while fleeing from Absalom. David's own son Absalom was conspiring against him to take over the kingship. Forced to flee from the palace, King David found himself in the middle of a desert wilderness. Many of us would be tempted to say to David that it would be appropriate for him to raise his fist to heaven and make a few demands to God. David did not do this. Instead, David found comfort and strength through meditating on God and His promises. He staked his claim and found solace. He remembered God. Spurgeon speaks of David's spiritual charisma when he writes, "There was no desert in his heart, though there was a desert around him." [5] Psalm 63 is rich in lessons, including some important claim-staking components of meditation that we all need to incorporate into our lives if we are to treasure God's promises.

Claim-staking Component #1: My Desire

Verses 1 and 2: O God, thou art my God; early will I seek thee: my soul thirsteth for thee, my flesh longeth for thee in a dry and thirsty land, where no water is; To see thy power and thy glory, so as I have seen thee in the sanctuary.

Meditating on God does not happen without a desire to seek God. Strong verbs comprise these verses: *seek, thirsteth*, and *longeth*. These verbs not only communicate a desire to be near God but also create a word picture of a passionate, yet desperate man who knows he needs God. David admits he is spiritually dehydrated; David also realizes that only God can satisfy. This verse has an important personal pronoun that gives David his foundation— "thou art MY God." David is claiming God as his own, and David is issuing a call for God's refreshment.

Why did David seek, thirst, and long for God? Because he wanted to see God's power and glory at work in his life. David wanted the Lord to show Himself real to David in the wilderness, just as the Lord had showed Himself real to David in the tabernacle. The wilderness had no churches, no sanctuaries, no tabernacles, and no prayer closets; but David knew from experience that the Lord was with him, whether in the tabernacle or in the wilderness. David asked for God's refreshment—His power and glory. We, like David, find refreshment from God through answered prayers and fulfilled promises that show God's glory and power.

Claim-staking Evaluating:
- Is God my God?
- Have I placed my trust in Christ to save me?
- Am I thirsty for God's refreshment?
- Do I long to grow?

- Am I willing to give part of my day to seek God?
- Am I desperate to know God?
- Would my family and friends consider me to be thirsty to know God and to grow in Him?
- Do I make note of answered prayers in my life, no matter how small the prayer may be?
- Can I see Christ at work in my heart outside the church building?
- Do I seek the Lord's working in my life outside church?

Claim-staking Component #2: My Worship
Verses 3 and 4: Because thy lovingkindness is better than life, my lips shall praise thee. Thus will I bless thee while I live: I will lift up my hands in thy name.

Lovingkindness, a word synonymous with *mercy* in the Old Testament, is the cause of David's worshipful praise to God. David knew of God's mercy personally. He sinned, God confronted him, David confessed, and God forgave. That mercy, David writes, is better than living or having breath. As a result of God's mercy, David praises Him and vows to bless God his entire life through the praise of his lips and the motions of his hands.

Claim-staking Evaluating:
- Do I view God only as the Judge and not the Mercy Giver?
- Have I experienced the mercy of God because I have confessed my sin and asked Him to forgive it?
- Do I proclaim God's kindness to me?
- Do I tend to praise God for the material things He supplies and fail to remember His kindness and mercy to my soul?
- Have I committed to praising God for the duration of my life?

Claim-staking Component #3: My Thoughts
Verses 5 and 6: My soul shall be satisfied as with marrow and fatness; and my mouth shall praise thee with joyful lips: When I remember thee upon my bed, and meditate on thee in the night watches.

The Greek word for *bed* in these verses is actually plural. The Greek reads, when David was on his "beds," he remembered God. David was a man on the run when he wrote this psalm. He had many beds, of which none were probably very comfortable considering his location in the wilderness. The words *night watches* also remind us that David was not safe. Guards were posted day and night; and David found himself staying up at night, most likely unable to sleep, because of the dangers, uncertainty, turmoil, challenges, and enemies that lurked just beyond his camp and threatened his family.

When I ponder David's situation, I am amazed at his focus. Instead of dwelling on his son's conspiracy, David pondered God's mercies. Instead of feeling sorry for his present sleeping conditions, David praised God. Instead of rehearsing in his mind what he was lacking, David remembered what he did have in God. Instead of being discontent with not having what he deserved, David found satisfaction in his God. Instead of allowing depression to take hold of him, David found reasons to joy in the Lord.

One small word in verse 5 made all the difference in David's life. We read this small word over and over again in the Psalm that David wrote. The word is *shall* or its twin counterpart *will*. David made a choice—I will be content; I will praise God. Throughout David's writing, we read of him making choices: I will trust, I will praise, I will declare, I will not be afraid, and so many other decisions of the will. David chose to think and remember his God. When life was hard, he chose to remember God. When life was uncomfortable, he chose to remember God. When life had many unknowns, he chose to remember God. When life hurt, he chose to remember God. When life did not make sense, he chose to remember God. That choice to remember God resulted in a satisfied, joyful life. Joyful living does not just happen; it is an emotional response to our beliefs. David continually made important choices about whom and what he was to believe. In the following verses, we can learn much from studying David's choices. Italics have been added for emphasis.

> Psalm 3:6—*I will not* be afraid of ten thousands of people, that have set themselves against me round about.

> Psalm 4:8—*I will* both lay me down in peace, and sleep: for thou, Lord, only makest me dwell in safety.

Psalm 7:17—*I will* praise the LORD according to his righteousness: and *will* sing praise to the name of the LORD most high.

Psalm 9:1-2—*I will* praise thee, O LORD, with my whole heart; *I will* shew forth all thy marvellous works. I will be glad and rejoice in thee: I will sing praise to thy name, O thou most High.

Psalm 13:6—*I will* sing unto the LORD, because he hath dealt bountifully with me.

Psalm 18:1-3—*I will* love thee, O LORD, my strength. The LORD is my rock, and my fortress, and my deliverer; my God, my strength, in whom *I will* trust; my buckler, and the horn of my salvation, and my high tower. *I will* call upon the LORD, who is worthy to be praised: so shall I be saved from mine enemies.

Psalm 22:22—*I will* declare thy name unto my brethren: in the midst of the congregation will I praise thee.

Psalm 23:4—Yea, though I walk through the valley of the shadow of death, *I will* fear no evil: for thou art with me; thy rod and thy staff they comfort me.

Psalm 26:11—But as for me, *I will* walk in mine integrity: redeem me, and be merciful unto me.

Psalm 27:6—And now shall mine head be lifted up above mine enemies round about me: therefore *will I* offer in his tabernacle sacrifices of joy; *I will* sing, yea, *I will* sing praises unto the LORD.

Psalm 30:1—*I will* extol thee, O LORD; for thou hast lifted me up, and hast not made my foes to rejoice over me.

Psalm 32:5—I acknowledged my sin unto thee, and mine iniquity have I not hid. I said, *I will* confess my transgressions unto the LORD; and thou forgavest the iniquity of my sin. Selah.

Psalm 34:1—*I will* bless the LORD at all times: his praise shall continually be in my mouth.

Psalm 38:18—For *I will* declare mine iniquity; *I will* be sorry for my sin.

Psalm 39:1—I said, *I will* take heed to my ways, that I sin not with my tongue: *I will* keep my mouth with a bridle, while the wicked is before me.

Psalm 52:9—*I will* praise thee for ever, because thou hast done it: and *I will* wait on thy name; for it is good before thy saints.

Psalm 56:3—What time I am afraid, *I will* trust in thee.

Psalm 86:7—In the day of my trouble *I will* call upon thee: for thou wilt answer me.

Psalm 86:11—Teach me thy way, O LORD; *I will* walk in thy truth: unite my heart to fear thy name.

Psalm 101:2-4—*I will* behave myself wisely in a perfect way. O when wilt thou come unto me? *I will* walk within my house with a perfect heart. *I will* set no wicked thing before mine eyes: I hate the work of them that turn aside; it shall not cleave to me. A froward heart shall depart from me: *I will* not know a wicked person.

Psalm 138:2—*I will* worship toward thy holy temple, and praise thy name for thy lovingkindness and for thy truth: for thou hast magnified thy word above all thy name.

Psalm 139:14—*I will* praise thee; for I am fearfully and wonderfully made: marvellous are thy works; and that my soul knoweth right well.

Psalm 144:9—*I will* sing a new song unto thee, O God: upon a psaltery and an instrument of ten strings *will I* sing praises unto thee.

Psalm 145:5—*I will* speak of the glorious honour of thy majesty, and of thy wondrous works.

Claim-staking Evaluating:

- Do my choices bring me joy or heartache?
- Have I found God satisfying?
- If not, could it be that I am not choosing to remember Him properly?
- Do I concentrate more on my present condition than on God's goodness to me?
- Whom or what do I think about first when life becomes difficult? Do I choose to believe and act upon God's promises?

Claim-staking Component #4: My Joy

Verses 7 and 8: Because thou hast been my help, therefore in the shadow of thy wings will I rejoice. My soul followeth hard after thee: thy right hand upholdeth me.

From Goliath to Saul to the Philistines at Gath to Absalom . . . God proved to David that He was David's Helper. In verse 7, David declares from experience that God helped him. Verses 7 and 8 list two ways that God specifically helped him: He protected David by placing David under His wing, and He upheld David with His power by lifting him with His hands. Protection and power—two promises that God fulfilled in David's life, time and time again. As a result of seeing God fulfill those promises in his life, David rejoiced and followed after God all the more.

I have often told the ladies in my Sunday school class that the more we know God, the more we will trust Him. The more we trust God, the easier it is to obey Him. The more we obey God, the more we realize how pleasurable it is to obey Him; therefore, we want to get to know Him better to discover the other benefits of knowing, trusting, and obeying Him. I call this cycle the KTO growth process—know, trust, obey.

In essence, David is proclaiming, "Because I know God has been my Helper, I am going to trust Him to protect and uphold me." As I see God fulfill His promises, I will rejoice and seek Him even more because what God says is true. He never fails me. There is no risk in trusting God.

Many times we live our Christian lives as if there are many risks to trusting God. But there are none. There may be sacrifices, but no risks. Staking our claim on God's promises only brings bounty to our lives.

Claim-staking Evaluating:
- Do I truly believe God keeps His promises?
- If so, are there some promises I have forgotten because I was too focused on getting through my hardship by myself?
- Have I taken note of God's protection and power in my life?
- Are these fulfilled promises forgotten?
- Should I write down those provisions to better remember how safe I am under God's wing and in His hand?
- Do I believe that trusting God is risky?
- If not, what keeps me from trusting Him more?
- What kinds of sacrifices might keep me from trusting and obeying God more?
- Do any of the sacrifices outweigh the benefit of obedience to God?

In review of these claim-staking components, we are reminded that David chose to meditate on God and His promises. He staked his claim on God's protection, power, and glory. Because God had shown Himself faithful before in the sanctuary and in the face of enemies, David had no doubt that God would continue to be faithful to him while he was in the wilderness and in the face of a rebelling son.

Treasuring God's promises begins with our staking our claim *by believing* and continues with our constant meditating *by thinking about God and His fulfilled promises.* In order to stake our claim and meditate, we have to know our claim. The more we know of God's promises, the more we can trust and believe them. The more we trust and believe, the more we discover that God does keep and fulfill His promises. The more we find of God to be true, the more we want to get to know Him.

Knowing the Treasure
Twice in 2 Peter, the author mentions the importance of knowledge: "Grace and peace be multiplied unto you **through the knowledge of God, and of Jesus our Lord**, According as his divine power hath given unto us all

things that pertain unto life and godliness, **through the knowledge of him that hath called us to glory and virtue**" (2 Peter 1:2-3). Now that we know that God highly treasures His promises, we must make getting to know those promises a priority in our lives. Through the knowledge of God, I have grace, peace, and the pertinent things I need to live a godly life.

To better get to know God and His promises, we can review the promises written in God's Word that I outlined in the section of this chapter on "Claiming Promises." We can then claim these promises and so many more that are in the Bible by

- getting to know God Who gives us all things that pertain to life and godliness,
- believing that God and His promises are true and relevant,
- finding specific promises in the Bible that relate to our lives today,
- memorizing verses that contain God's promises, and
- praying these promises back to God, especially when the doubts and temptations arise in our hearts.

When we apply God's promises to our lives, we become partakers of the divine nature, which is endless in benefits and blessings. These great and precious promises are ours to claim. They are ours to value. May we learn to value what God values.

You Can't Stand on Promises

You can go to church twice on Sundays; make the Wednesday service, too.
You don't even need a songbook to sing hymn one forty two.
You can sing "Standing on the Promises" and repeat the last four bars,
But you can't stand on promises if you don't know what they are.

You've listened to a thousand sermons, but you never really heard
That the only way your life will change is to get into God's Word.
You can try to walk on water, but you'll never get too far.
'Cause you can't stand on promises if you don't know what they are.

If there's a trip to the Holy Land, you'll be the first to go.
You give ten dollars to the mission field, and let everybody know.
Your service as an usher outshines the brightest star,
But you can't stand on promises if you don't know what they are.

Well, you raised your hand, and you met the Lord over twenty years ago.
But John 3:16 and Psalm 23 are the only verses you know.
I can see why things aren't working; why things aren't up to par
'Cause you can't stand on promises if you don't know what they are.

--Greg Nelson, James Isaac Elliott, and Phil McHugh [6]

THE WORTH OF THIS TREASURE

2 Peter 1:4

Whereby are given unto us exceeding great and precious promises: that by these ye might be partakers of the divine nature, having escaped the corruption that is in the world through lust.

- Its Origin: From God; we partake by faith through divine grace
- Its Purpose: For God to show Himself faithful to us; so that we can experience the abundance of God's storehouse of love
- Its Potential: We become partakers of the divine nature

What keeps me from valuing God's promises? Not believing; not meditating; not knowing.

*His
Lovingkindness* 6

Psalm 36:7

How excellent is thy lovingkindness, O God!
therefore the children of men put their trust
under the shadow of thy wings.

While I was growing up, my family did a lot of tent camping for our vacations. Those weeks became highlights of our year and now provide lively conversation during family gatherings as we recall the different events that occurred during those camping trips. The weather was always an uncertain element in our planned trips. Back then, we did not have access to weather channels or internet sources to tell us the upcoming forecast for a specific region. I am thankful that my dad was the master comfort camper and had tarps jerry-rigged throughout our campsite to shelter us from the elements. Those tarps not only provided protection during hostile downpours of rain but also gave comfort and pleasure during the hottest parts of the day. We congregated under the shade of the tarps by day and found the fellowship and relaxation sweet, and we gathered under the protection of the tarps by night when the rain came down so hard that our tents leaked. The tarps' cover was a much welcome relief, but they only protected us and provided shade for us when we were under them. When we moved from under their shadow, we were exposed to the elements. I experienced many rainy trips to the outhouse where I wished my dad had continued his tarp jerry-rigging all the way to that building.

God's Nest of Protection and Provision

David uses a beautiful word picture in Psalm 36:7-8: "How excellent is thy lovingkindness, O God! therefore the children of men put their trust under the shadow of thy wings. They shall be abundantly satisfied with the fatness of thy house; and thou shalt make them drink of the river of thy pleasures." Whether the wings in the verse speak of the cherubim wings that overshadowed the mercy seat during David's time or whether they speak of a bird's wings that protect her young, we have a beautiful picture of trust and safety that is a result of God's faithful kindness. These verses show us God's kindness not only in how He protects us but also in how He cares for us. We are "abundantly satisfied" as a result of being in God's presence and

89

drinking of God's pleasures. God wants to protect, and He wants to provide. These verses clearly declare that God's kindness is precious and that God has pleasure in showing His kindness by protecting and providing for those who trust Him. Where else would I want to be than safe and warm in God's presence? In the same way I found comfort and protection under my dad's tarps, I, as God's child, can find comfort and protection under the wings of His lovingkindness.

The word *excellent* in Psalm 36:7 means precious, honorable, and costly. The Hebrew word comes from a root word that means to prize or to make rare. David through God's inspiration is declaring that God's lovingkindness is a valuable treasure. Because of God's precious kindness, we can rest in the shadow of God's wings.

Some may have heard the illustration of the barn fire that ravaged a small farm on the outskirts of town. Shortly after the fire was put out, the farmer walked around his property checking to see what livestock had survived the blaze. The chicken coop behind the barn was a heap of ash. With sadness, the farmer bent down in the corner of the coop and found a severely charred hen. As he looked down at the mother bird, he noticed movement underneath her burnt remains. The farmer was astounded to find baby chicks safely under their dead mother. Despite the intensity of the flame, the hen never ran for her own safety. Her chicks were more important to her, and she kept them safe under her wings, despite the dangers all around her.

We often hear this familiar story compared to God's protection of us and Christ's sacrifice on the cross for us. But just as the chicks were safe under the mother hen's wings and just as my family was safe under my dad's tarps, so we as God's children are safe *under* God's wings, not on top, but under our heavenly Father's wings. We find protection in the shadow of God. According to Psalm 36:7, my *position* is important to my *protection*.

If ever we find ourselves thinking we can survive outside the shadows of God's winged protection, we become foolishly exposed to the elements of this world and the sinful temptations that the world rains down on us. In God's enduring kindness, He has covered us with His wings of safety and provision. If we find ourselves beaten down or in sin, we have to conclude based on God's Word that God's protection never moved; but rather, we foolishly walked out from under His gracious tarps that sheltered us from the elements. The moment I think I can stay dry outside God's tarps despite sin's downpour all around me, I have moved toward pride's self-destruction and farther away from God's grace that is protecting me.

My position is important, and I am foolish to think that walking away from God's lovingkindness is harmless. I need to trust His tarps, His wings, His kindness in my life. God's nest of protection and provision are under His wings. God is a kind God Who wants to protect and care for His children, if only I will let Him.

God's Precious Lovingkindness

When I am exposed to God's kindness every day and am made aware that God orchestrates the different avenues of goodness in my life, then I find it very difficult to turn my back on God. Nevertheless, there is always the temptation to doubt God's love. I am grateful to my parents, who time and time again throughout my childhood, reminded me that God was very in-volved in my circumstances. When I did not see life's events as good things, my parents made me aware of God's presence and His goodness, despite my poor perceptions. I needed those reminders then, and I need those remind-ers today. We forget about God's kindness. The children of Israel forgot, and their forgetfulness led them down a path of self-destruction. By remem-bering God's goodness—especially His patience and mercy in my life—I am reminded of what I would be without Christ, and I am humbled by the thought. As parents, we sometimes think that hard-knock discipline is the only way our children will "come around" or "repent of their sins" when, by example, the Lord shows us that lovingkindness is the softener of a hard heart.

The Hebrew word in the Old Testament *checed* (also written as *hesed* and pronounced *kheh séd*) means kindness, favor, and mercy; but *checed* is trans-lated in the King James Version using several different English words such as *mercy, lovingkindness, goodness*, and *merciful kindness*. The Greek word in the New Testament *chrestos* or *chrestotes* means kindness, moral excellence, and gentleness. Similar to the Old Testament Hebrew word *checed*, the New Tes-tament Greek word *chrestos* is translated in the King James Version using several different English words such as *kindness, gentleness, easy,* and *gracious.* The Bible uses many different words to convey God's kindness.

As I studied the passages that characterize God's kindness, I discovered and then tried to comprehend the value of His kindness in my life. I began to better understand why God calls His lovingkindness precious. Below is a list of some benefits of God's lovingkindness in the lives of His children.

God's kindness leads me to repentance.

Romans 2:4—Or despisest thou the riches of his **goodness** and forbearance and longsuffering; not knowing that the **goodness** of God leadeth thee to repentance?

God's kindness causes me to trust Him more.

Psalm 36:7-8—How excellent is thy **lovingkindness**, O God! therefore the children of men put their trust under the shadow of thy wings. They shall be abundantly satisfied with the fatness of thy house; and thou shalt make them drink of the river of thy pleasures.

God's kindness revives me.

Psalm 119:88—Quicken me after thy **lovingkindness**; so shall I keep the testimony of thy mouth.

Psalm 119:159—Consider how I love thy precepts: quicken me, O LORD according to thy **lovingkindness**.

God's kindness makes me want more of Him.

Jeremiah 31:3—The LORD hath appeared of old unto me, saying, Yea, I have loved thee with an everlasting love: therefore with **lovingkindness** have I drawn thee.

God's kindness sustains me.

Psalm 94:17-18—Unless the LORD had been my help, my soul had almost dwelt in silence. When I said, My foot slippeth; thy **mercy**, O LORD, held me up.

God's kindness gives me joyful lips.

Psalm 63:3-5—Because thy **lovingkindness** is better than life, my lips shall praise thee. Thus will I bless thee while I live: I will lift up my hands in thy name. My soul shall be satisfied as with marrow and fatness; and my mouth shall praise thee with joyful lips:

God's kindness comforts me.

Psalm 119:76-77—Let, I pray thee, thy **merciful kindness** be for my comfort, according to thy word unto thy servant. Let thy tender mercies come unto me, that I may live: for thy law is my delight.

God's kindness preserves me.

Lamentations 3:22-23—It is of the LORD's **mercies** that we are not consumed, because his compassions fail not. They are new every morning: great is thy faithfulness.

From my own Christian life experiences, I can say that I have been humbled to repentance by God's lovingkindness; I have found trusting God easier by remembering His lovingkindness; I have been renewed in spirit and body by meditating on God's lovingkindness; and I have found a yearning to know God more because of His constant lovingkindness He has shed on me. But He does all of this and more.

God says that His lovingkindness is precious and should be precious to me. Why? Because it sustains, comforts, and preserves me and because it causes me to repent, to trust, to be revived, to grow closer to God, and to praise Him with joyful lips. When I comprehend these truths, how can I not value His lovingkindness in my life?

Loyal Love

I have asked audiences of all ages what they believe to be one of the most important traits in a friendship. The number one answer is usually love, but a close second answer is loyalty. Considered to be an important element in a thriving friendship, loyalty or the lack of it can make or break a friendship. During my word study of *lovingkindness*, the words *mercy* and *loyalty* often surfaced on the pages of my reading. Lovingkindness is a steadfast love that is loyal and merciful.[1]

Our idea of loyalty in a friendship is often defined by what is said, what is done, and what is kept. During a child's upper elementary to high school years, we may hear him say that a friend is loyal if he does not say bad things about him, if he plays with him, or if he keeps secrets or his promises. God is loyal to us, but His loyalty is not blind loyalty that says, "No matter what, I'll stand by you." This type of loyalty is dangerous and often requires a person to be disloyal to a more important cause. God is not loyal to me while being disloyal to His deity.

If I tell a person that I will stand by him no matter what, and then I find out that standing by him means I have to stand against God and His Word, then my loyalty to one person becomes more important than my loyalty to God. The Bible term for this is idolatry. Any thing or person, including blind loyalty, that is more important to me than God is, is an idol in my life (Ezekiel 14).

So, is God loyal? Yes! He *is* loyal to me. His loyalty is just one aspect of His lovingkindness toward me. He loyally loves me each and every day of my life. How does God show His loyal love to me?

By telling me the truth

Deuteronomy 32:4—He is the Rock, his work is perfect: for all his ways are judgment: a God of truth and without iniquity, just and right is he.

By thinking precious thoughts toward me

Psalm 139:17—How precious also are thy thoughts unto me, O God! how great is the sum of them!

Psalm 40:5—Many, O LORD my God, are thy wonderful works which thou hast done, and thy thoughts which are to us-ward: they cannot be reckoned up in order unto thee: if I would declare and speak of them, they are more than can be numbered.

By never leaving me nor forsaking me

Hebrews 13:5—Let your conversation be without covetousness; and be content with such things as ye have: for he hath said, I will never leave thee, nor forsake thee.

By keeping His promises

Deuteronomy 7:8-9—But because the LORD loved you, and because he would keep the oath which he had sworn unto your fathers, hath the LORD brought you out with a mighty hand, and redeemed you out of the house of bondmen, from the hand of Pharaoh king of Egypt. Know therefore that the LORD thy God, he is God, the faithful God, which keepeth covenant and mercy with them that love him and keep his commandments to a thousand generations.

By taking a firm stand against sin and offering me an escape

Romans 6:6—Knowing this, that our old man is crucified with him, that the body of sin might be destroyed, that henceforth we should not serve sin.

1 Corinthians 10:13—There hath no temptation taken you but such as is common to man: but God is faithful, who will not suffer you to be tempted above that ye are able; but will with the temptation also make a way to escape, that ye may be able to bear it.

By knowing my secrets and still loving me

Psalm 139:23-24 Search me, O God, and know my heart: try me, and know my thoughts: And see if there be any wicked way in me, and lead me in the way everlasting.

Psalm 44:21—Shall not God search this out? for he knoweth the secrets of the heart.

By forgiving me

Psalm 103:12—As far as the east is from the west, so far hath he removed our transgressions from us.

1 John 1:9—If we confess our sins, he is faithful and just to forgive us our sins, and to cleanse us from all unrighteousness.

By giving me a confident hope

Jeremiah 29:11—For I know the thoughts that I think toward you, saith the LORD, thoughts of peace, and not of evil, to give you an expected end.

Kindness, An Act of Love

God is kind because God is love. There is no question in Scripture as to which came first—God's kindness or God's love. Kindness is clearly an act of love. Jeremiah 31:3 speaks first about God's everlasting love and then speaks of His kindness drawing us. "The LORD hath appeared of old unto me, saying, Yea, I have loved thee with an everlasting love: therefore with lovingkindness have I drawn thee."Titus 3 speaks of God's kindness and love, and Ephesians 2 speaks of God's mercy and love. 1 John has many verses that tell us about God's love and the kindness He bestows on us *because* He loves us. Without love, there is no sincere kindness. Because God loves me, He is kind to me.

When I say the word *lovingkindness* over and over again to try to get my limited knowledge of language around the word, I conclude that when Darby termed the English word *lovingkindness* as a good English translation for *checed*, he put much thought into the word. God bestows not just any kindness; He bestows *loving* kindness. In other words, He loves being kind. God's kindness is loving, and His loving is kindness.

I believe it is possible to be kind to someone without loving that person. People across the United States of America are kind to others whom they have not met. This is evidenced by the hundreds of charities that Americans support without ever knowing the people they help. I also believe that a person can love another but not always be kind. We see this phenomenon in a number of relationships just within the family. With God, we get to experience the complete package. God is love, and He manifested His kindness to us in the person Jesus Christ. Lovingkindness, both love and kindness, is one of God's treasures He gives to us.

I can better treasure this lovingkindness by learning to emulate God's example. Do I love kindness? Is my kindness loving, or is it just a duty? Do I show my love to others by my kindness to them? Am I being sincerely kind? If I fail in any of these areas, I need to go back to whether I am truly loving God the way I ought to love Him.

Treasuring Lovingkindness

So how can we better value this priceless treasure? God's love extends to us through His kindness. Love and kindness work side by side, according to Titus 3:4, in giving us a way of salvation through Jesus Christ. God shows His love by His kindness, and He showers us with kindness because of His love. Both the resulting work of Calvary and the lovingkindness that Christ performed on the cross and within our hearts are precious to God.

We know why this lovingkindness is precious to God and should be precious to us. But how can we better value this lovingkindness in our lives? There is no better textbook that tells us how than the Word of God. We can treasure God's steadfast love to us by

1. Proclaiming it

Psalm 59:16—But I will sing of thy power; yea, I will **sing aloud of thy mercy** in the morning: for thou hast been my defence and refuge in the day of my trouble.

Psalm 89:1—I will **sing of the mercies** of the LORD for ever: with my mouth will I make known thy faithfulness to all generations.

Psalm 92:1-4—It is a good thing to give thanks unto the LORD, and to sing praises unto thy name, O most High: To **shew forth thy loving-kindness** in the morning, and thy faithfulness every night, Upon an instrument of ten strings, and upon the psaltery; upon the harp with a solemn sound. For thou, LORD, hast made me glad through thy work: I will triumph in the works of thy hands.

Psalm 101:1—**I will sing of mercy** and judgment: unto thee, O LORD, will I sing.

How can I proclaim God's kindness in my life? According to the above verses, one of the best ways to proclaim God's kindness is to sing about His kindness. Whether in corporate worship, in the privacy of our homes, or in the confines of our cars, we can sing aloud about God's kindness. When we take the time to evaluate the songs that we sing, we can better determine whether we are proclaiming God's kindness. Music is one of the avenues we can use to meditate on how God has been good to us.

2. Thanking God for it

Psalm 136:1-3—**O give thanks unto the LORD**; for he is good: for his mercy endureth for ever. **O give thanks unto the God of gods**: for his mercy endureth for ever. **O give thanks to the Lord of lords**: for his mercy endureth for ever.

There are numerous verses that tell us we need to be thankful because of God's *checed* in our lives. We have much to be thankful for, but I find in my life that it is not enough to just be thankful. I need to verbalize my gratitude to God in my prayers and in sharing my testimony of God's lovingkindness to others. God wants to hear us *say* we are thankful to Him.

3. Thinking on it
Psalm 48:9—We have **thought of thy lovingkindness**, O God, in the midst of thy temple.

The word thought in this verse means to compare or consider. "I considered God's lovingkindness" is one way of paraphrasing this verse. The psalmist is saying that when he is worshiping the Lord, he is pondering, using comparisons or similitude, and thinking about God's goodness in his life. When I think and meditate on a passage and begin to understand and formulate word pictures and apply the verse to my own life, I better grasp the value of the truth or principle in the verse. It becomes more personal. God wants us to make His lovingkindness in our lives a personal treasure. When we have thought on His goodness, meditated on what it means in our lives, grasped its full measure, found ways to describe it to others, and discovered its reality in our lives, then we have "thought" well on His lovingkindness.

4. Regarding it
Psalm 143:8—Cause me to **hear thy lovingkindness** in the morning; for in thee do I trust: cause me to know the way wherein I should walk; for I lift up my soul unto thee.

The word *hear* in Psalm 143:8 speaks of regarding intelligently or giving attention to something, which specifically in this verse is God's lovingkindness. When I was growing up, my parents made sure that I "heard" of God's goodness as they reminded me over and over that the events in my life were allowed by God and were (and continue to be) an act of His goodness in my life. I remember vividly the dinner-table talks where my dad would rehearse blessings and answered prayers to us and remind us that God is good. I also remember those more difficult days when the loss of a loved one, a financial strain, or an illness would rock our lives. My dad still rehearsed to us that God was doing a good work in our lives. All along, without my knowing it then, I was "hearing" of God's lovingkindness from my dad. I learned to regard each event in my life as an act of God's goodness. I did not always understand the event nor did I always see good in the event, but I had to believe the event was for my good because God's promises never fail. This belief is the essence of faith. Not only can I treasure lovingkindness by regarding it in and throughout my life, but also I can value it by rehearsing God's goodness to my family and co-workers. Psalm 84:11 promises "that no good thing will He withhold from them that walk uprightly."

5. Loving it

Micah 6:8—He hath shewed thee, O man, what is good; and what doth the Lord require of thee, but to do justly, and to **love mercy**, and to walk humbly with thy God?

The more I meditate on this verse, the more I realize that the English phrase "love mercy" is very close to "loving kindness." The word *love* in this verse refers to an affectionate love. Affectionate love is an outward display of desire. I tell my Sunday school class that compassion is not really compassion without action. I might say I want to help someone, but until I actually perform a helpful act to that person, the desire is only a nice thought. In much of the same sense, I might say that I love to be kind and merciful; but until I begin to perform acts of kindness or mercy, the desire is only a nice thought. For instance, if I say I love mercy and want to be kind, then the next time someone hurts me, I need to be ready to forgive. Loving mercy is *being* merciful by forgiving. Do I affectionately love mercy by showing mercy to others?

6. Trusting it

Psalm 13:5-6—But I have **trusted in thy mercy**; my heart shall rejoice in thy salvation. I will sing unto the Lord, because he hath dealt bountifully with me.

The best way we can trust in God's kindness is to take God at His Word through obedience. If God's lovingkindness offers me protection under

God's wings, then I rest in this promise and obey. There is no better evidence of trust than obedience. I treasure God's lovingkindness when I begin to seek to obey God. Psalm 13 and John 15 have one common vein: they both tell us that joy is a result of depending on and obeying God.

God's lovingkindness is excellent, is precious. Christ's death, burial, and resurrection were acts of lovingkindness. Christ's preparing a mansion for me in heaven is an act of lovingkindness. Christ's forgiveness of my sins is an act of lovingkindness. We cannot put a price tag on this love and kindness. We need to value it, to treasure it.

What More Can You Ask

God's love endureth forever—
What a wonderful thing to know
When the tides of life run against you
And your spirit is downcast and low . . .
God's kindness is ever around you,
Always ready to freely impart
Strength to your faltering spirit,
Cheer to your lonely heart . . .
God's presence is ever beside you,
As near as the reach of your hand,
You have but to tell Him your troubles,
There is nothing He won't understand . . .
And knowing God's love is unfailing,
And His mercy unending and great,
You have but to trust in His promise—
"God comes not too soon or too late" . . .
So wait with a heart that is patient
For the goodness of God to prevail—
For never do prayers go unanswered,
And His mercy and love never fail.

--Helen Steiner Rice[2]

THE WORTH OF THIS TREASURE

Psalm 36:7

How excellent is thy lovingkindness, O God! therefore the children of men put their trust under the shadow of thy wings.

- Its Origin: God is love, and God loves us.
- Its Purpose: To draw us to God; an outward display of God's love
- Its Potential: I am a recipient of God's goodness which is limitless

What keeps me from valuing His lovingkindness? My pride as I move away from God's protection and power.

The Death
of a Saint 7

As a Christian, my earthly death is my eternal entrance into the very presence of God. We have heard this truth taught numerous times during funerals or Sunday services, and I find comfort in the simple but profound truth that God considers my entering into His presence precious. I can fathom the idea that as a Christian I should look forward to being in God's presence in heaven someday, but the psalmist in Psalm 116 writes that God is looking forward to *my* being in His presence so much so that my death is a precious thing in His sight. Because I am redeemed with the precious blood of Christ and am made a saint through Christ, my physical death becomes precious to the Lord because He can now receive my soul for eternity.

If I am to learn to value what God values, I need to learn to value the death of His saints. Furthermore, as a child of God, I need to remember that my own death is a treasure to God. The word *saint* in Psalm 116:15 is not referring to the traditional Catholic definition where one earns sainthood based on his life's contributions. The word *saint* in Psalm 116:15 is referring to a person whom God has sanctified and set apart through the precious blood of His Son Jesus Christ. A saint is one of His children, a sanctified sinner. There is no committee that deems me a saint; I cannot become a saint based on my own merit. God declared me a saint, holy and godly before Him, when He justified me through Jesus' work on Calvary.

> Romans 5:8-11—But God commendeth his love toward us, in that, while we were yet sinners, Christ died for us. Much more then, being now justified by his blood, we shall be saved from wrath through him. For if, when we were enemies, we were reconciled to God by the death of his Son, much more, being reconciled, we shall be saved by his life. And not only so, but we also joy in God through our Lord Jesus Christ, by whom we have now received the atonement.

I was an enemy of God until I was saved and given an inheritance in Him. My death will place me before the throne of God where I will experience firsthand the good pleasures of His inheritance. I look forward to that; but

God, even more so, considers that moment to be precious, honorable, valuable. He anticipates my being with Him, too.

A Philippian Path to Peace

Facing death is never easy, whether we are the one dying or the one being left behind. In recent months I have had to say goodbye to a grandmother (my mom's mother) and to a grandfather (my dad's father). Both were saints, sanctified sinners in Christ; and both were my heroes. Facing their deaths has been some of the most heart-wrenching moments of my life. I did not realize how their deaths would test my faith. I knew my grandparents were in a better place. I knew they were no longer hurting. I knew with time my pain would heal and life would continue. I did not doubt God's ability to comfort and care for those of us left behind, but the loss was not easy.

My faith was tested in how I viewed my grandparents' earthly bodies after their deaths. I found it difficult to walk away from my grandpa's gravesite or to know my grandma's body was being flown across the country, and I was not with her. A part of me would rehearse verses and songs that reminded me that the soul lives forever in heaven, but the other part of me pictured my loved ones alone in a coffin with mounds of dirt over them. Those moments were hard to face. The grief is real, but so is our hope, if only we choose to hope.

Our thoughts can help us heal as we ponder the sweet memories of our loved ones, but our thoughts can also slow the healing process if they are not grounded in the truth of God's Word. Paul reminds us of the importance of our thought life.

> Philippians 4:6-9—Be careful for nothing; but in every thing by prayer and supplication with thanksgiving let your requests be made known unto God. And the peace of God, which passeth all understanding, shall keep your hearts and minds through Christ Jesus. Finally, brethren, whatsoever things are true, whatsoever things are honest, whatsoever things are just, whatsoever things are pure, whatsoever things are lovely, whatsoever things are of good report; if there be any virtue, and if there be any praise, think on these things. Those things, which ye have both learned, and received, and heard, and seen in me, do: and the God of peace shall be with you.

I call this passage in Philippians "The Philippian Path to Peace." These verses have commands that we should adhere to in order for us to experience the peace of God. First, I do not need to be anxious about anything. Second, I need to tell God with a thankful attitude what is going on in my life. Third, I need to think on things that are truthful, honorable, right, clean, acceptable, reputable, excellent, and commendable. Fourth, I need to study Paul's life and God-inspired teaching, learn from them, and then do (put to practice) what I have learned. These are four basic steps toward peace, according to Philippians 4.

I usually do not journal, but the days following my grandfather's death were filled with so many faith-building episodes that I had to put on paper how the Lord was helping and teaching me to grieve. I wrote these events in journal-style, and in doing so wanted to practically apply "The Philippian Path to Peace" verses to my life. The events are recorded below; my response to those events is in italics. I share them with my readers for no other purpose than to praise the Lord for what He has taught me.

Tuesday, August 8, 2006

I have visited my grandparents, who are also my neighbors, nearly every day for the past ten years. My grandpa's failing health in the last year and a half has given me the opportunity to minister to my grandparents as I have cooked, cleaned, bathed, clothed, and shopped for them. Although tiring, I have considered these opportunities honorable. Now as I near a two-and-a-half-week vacation, I am mindful that I may never see my grandpa again. The thought lingers in my mind as I say goodbye to him. I give him a big hug, tell him to be good to his wife and to keep smiling. My grandpa's mental health is not as sharp as it used to be, but he still knew me and called me by name. "Sweetheart," he said, "you make sure you come back to us. We need you. I don't know what it would be like without you. I love you." Upon hearing those words, I told him I loved him too and left the room to finish packing for the plane ride to Denver.

I know there is nothing to worry about. God is with Grandpa. He will take care of Grandpa better than I ever could. Lord, I have a long trip ahead of me. Please watch over my grandparents and my family as we are apart. Thank you for giving me the opportunity to visit family and thank you for folks who are willing to care for my grandparents while I am away. Thank you for this opportunity to lean on You.

Wednesday, August 9, 2006

Steve and I pack up our kids and head to the Las Vegas airport for our plane trip to Denver to visit my brother Daniel and his family. We have friends who live in Las Vegas, and they volunteer to park our Suburban at their home so we don't have to pay for parking at the airport.

Saturday, August 12, 2006

I call Grandma to see how she and Grandpa are doing. I update her on our visit and let her know how the kids are getting along with their cousins. Grandma informs me they are doing as well as expected. I ask Grandma to give Grandpa an "I love you" message and then I hang up with her. So far, our vacation is going well, and we soon begin switching gears for our next flight scheduled for early Monday morning to visit family in the Midwest.

Sunday, August 13, 2006

7:30 a.m.

I get up and begin getting ready for church. Shortly after 8:00 a.m. and as I am applying the finishing touches to my face to look presentable at church, I hear the phone ring. Moments later, Daniel knocks on the door; I open it; and he informs me that Mom called to tell us that Grandpa had died in the night. Shock. Pain. Loss. Tears. Memories of my last conversation with him. Unknowns. Vacation plans. Telling my children that their great-grandpa is gone. Major upcoming changes. Heaven. Relief. Sadness. Not being there for Grandpa. Not being there for Grandma. All of these emotions and thoughts began running through my head.

Lord, I have no idea why You chose to take Grandpa home during my vacation. I know Your timing is best, but right now, it appears so difficult. Steve and the kids have been looking forward to seeing family in the Midwest, but now

I know a funeral will take us back home. There is no question about what is right and honorable to do, but the "double whammy" disappointment of losing Grandpa plus not seeing family we had planned to see is hard for children to understand. Lord, please prepare my children's hearts and my husband's heart for this news. Give my husband wisdom in knowing what the next step will be for our family. Lord, Grandma needs You more than ever. Make Yourself real to her. Thank you for friends and family that are already surrounding her with Your love. Lord, I know I need to think on things that are true, honorable, and acceptable. Keep my thoughts stayed on Thee, for I need Your peace this hour and for the many hard hours to come. Thank you for welcoming my Grandpa with open arms. He so much wanted to see You face to face. Grandpa loved his Sundays. Without a doubt, this Sunday will forever be my Grandpa's best Sunday ever!

8:30 a.m.

After absorbing the news of Grandpa's death, I return to the guest bedroom to share the news with Steve. He took the news quietly. Grandpa treated Steve like a grandson, and my grandparents told me often how thankful they were for Steve as their neighbor and grandson-in-law. I know that Steve was battling the grief of my grandpa's loss, but also trying to figure out what that meant for the rest of our vacation. (His side of the family lives in the Midwest.) He knew, even as I did, that the delicate conversation had to include the importance of returning to honor a godly man (who for years showed me his love in many tangible ways) as well as the proper stewardship of plane tickets and other responsibilities. (We had scheduled a deputation visit in a church in Wisconsin for the coming Wednesday.) We decided to not be hasty in our decisions and to go to church. We would make decisions and tell our children after church.

Lord, there are so many unknowns. I have to trust You to work out the details, but we need Your discernment. I want to honor my grandpa, but I want my children to spend time with Steve. And Steve, he has looked forward to seeing his family for so long. Lord, please show us how we can do both. Thank you for doing what is best in our lives. Going to church will help us keep our thoughts on You.

12:30 p.m.

We return to my brother's home and there in the guest room Steve informs our children of Grandpa's death. They, of course, ask many questions. More questions than we had answers. But to my amazement, they didn't ask questions about where Grandpa was. Instead, they made statements. "Mom," Courtney, my six-year-old, says, "Grandpa is in heaven and his body is just right." "Grandpa is in a better place now, Mom," Clay, my seven-year-old, says. Devon, with tears in his eyes, tells me he'll miss Grandpa. What precious moments to a mom! My faith was strengthened through my children's unwavering faith.

Lord, thank you for a family that reminds me of truths that are honest, right, clean, acceptable, and reputable. Oh, how I needed to hear the strong faith of my children and to hurt alongside them in the loss of Grandpa. Thank you, thank you, thank you, Lord. You knew exactly what I needed, although it was hard to do. Your grace far out-muscled my weaknesses. You, Lord, have shown Yourself faithful. Continue to keep Your promises as we work out the details for the upcoming days.

1:30 p.m.

The cousins (ages ranging from four to nine) find comfort in talking to each other about Great-Grandpa. While we try to eat some lunch, Steve and I, along with Daniel and Esther, have a powwow around the lunch table to discuss the next step. Steve had made several phone calls to the airlines before church and after church to see what they would allow us to do in the area of switching flight times and locations. The bottom-line results of those phone calls weren't promising. The airlines would do nothing unless we personally saw a ticket agent at the airport. I called Mom to find out the details of the funeral. They didn't have anything set in stone because the coroner had just left, and the funeral home didn't want to commit until Monday morning. More unknowns. Mom was able to give us a few possible scenarios, but she couldn't verify or confirm anything without first hearing from the funeral home. The next step became clear to us: we needed to travel to the Denver airport to talk with an airline agent in person.

4:00 p.m.

We arrive at the airport and find what we think is the correct line to be in to ask our questions, and we quietly wait with reserved hope that something could be done. Based on the phone conversations with the airlines earlier, we expected to be able to have our tickets changed but pay a fine for each ticket. We had presented every scenario possible, but it seemed the only reasonable one to pursue would be to try to get our ticket changed from Monday to Thursday afternoon. This meant that we would have to travel by car back to California (14 hours) on Monday, attend the viewing on Tuesday, the burial service on Wednesday morning, and the memorial on Wednesday afternoon. We then would need to travel all night back to Denver to catch the early afternoon flight to Chicago on Thursday. The entire plan not only sounded exhausting but it would be exhausting. But we knew this seemed to be the best situation for our family and Daniel's family. We had peace about the tiring plan, but we needed the airlines to cooperate, and we needed the plane to be empty enough to place five new passengers on the flight. August flights are routinely full because it is one of the more popular vacationing months. Bottom line—we needed a miracle.

4:05 p.m.

We continue to stand in line. We couldn't help but observe the ticket agent who was helping the folks in front of us. We become discouraged as we realize this particular airline agent is having a very bad day according to her outward expressions and unwillingness to help. I begin to pray earnestly.

4:10 p.m.

We finally get to the front of the line at the airport. We had just spent ten minutes waiting in line watching the mannerisms of the ticket agent. Unfortunately for us, her mannerisms and facial expressions don't give us much confidence of a hopeful expectation. I keep praying as Steve and I step toward her.

Lord, I won't worry about this because you have something planned for us that will be in our best interest, but if this lady holds the key to our getting

to California for a funeral plus getting to the Midwest for the rest of our va-
cation then you're going to have to do some "attitude checks" with her. She is
sourpuss already even before we have asked her anything! But Lord, I forgot, I
must think on things that are clean and right. Even though this lady's outside
demeanor says one thing, I will change my thoughts to expecting great things
from You. You, so much more than this ticket lady, are reputable. But Lord, we
need her on our side. Do what You do best.

4:11 p.m.

Steve begins sharing our situation with the sourpuss ticket lady. She
doesn't say a word, nor does she smile or sympathize with our situation. But Steve keeps talking. We then present our request to her. She
takes our tickets. Still, she has not said a word nor smiled. She begins
typing on her computer. Still, no word and no smile. No sympathy.
No indication that she even heard our request. We wait. We pray. We
do more waiting. She says nothing.

Then she speaks, "The flight you requested on Thursday is available.
When you return, you will need to show proof that you attended
a funeral. Failure to do so will result in a fine. Here are your new
tickets." She can speak! She handed us our new tickets and then said,
"By the way, you were in the wrong line. Next time please use the
line over there." She points to a long line of people not more than
twenty feet away from us. We knew immediately that everything that
just happened was of God! God took care of us despite our mistakes.
With new tickets in hand, we head back to Daniel's home to work out
the "ground transportation" and to pack for a quick trip home and a
quick turnaround for Thursday's plane trip.

Paul writes that God's grace is sufficient, that God's strength is perfected even
in our weakness, and that God's peace passes all understanding. Lord, keep
reminding me of Your Words. They are true, and they are faithful. Thank you,
Lord. Oh, and Lord, thank you for letting me smile even when I'm hurting
deep down inside.

Monday, August 14, 2006
4:30 a.m.

We begin our trip back to California with my brother's two cars. He and his family are in his little red car, and Steve and I and our three children are in the family van. We make good progress and find ourselves about 250 miles outside Las Vegas, making us roughly 6 hours from home. The trip is moving along smoothly when, all of a sudden, we heard, "clank, clank, clunk, clunk" coming from the van. Using my cell phone, I call Daniel in the car ahead of us, and Steve begins to slow down. We took the next exit off the interstate.

11:30 a.m.

Forty miles from Cedar City, Utah, we found ourselves stuck on an off ramp with no feasible solution for a quick return to the interstate. While the guys lifted the hood to try to diagnose what we were hoping would be obvious and simple to fix, I pulled out my AAA card so Steve could make the call. I love my brother and husband, but they were not gifted with mechanical skills so the AAA card became a necessity. We had been traveling about seven hours, just slightly beyond the halfway point. We tried to find some humor in the situation, and even joke about driving the van onto the car carrier that was parked ahead of us on the same off ramp. The humor fades when Steve gets off the phone with AAA and informs us that we only have twenty-mile towing so we would have to pay the extra towing fees to go to Cedar City unless we wanted to back track to the small town we just passed. How much more bad news could we handle!

By this time, the driver in the car carrier notices us behind him, and he steps out of his 18-wheeler and meanders to our 2-car caravan. Steve and Daniel inform him of our situation, and the driver yanks on his greasy gloves and begins to check out the engine. He shakes his head, pulls off his greasy gloves, and tells us there isn't much use in even getting the van fixed. The engine is most likely blown and would cost more than the value of the van. More bad news!

Lord, do You see My situation? Do You see six children running around the Utah desert expending energy and my trying to keep them from asking nag-

ging questions that the dads don't have answers for? Do You feel the heat? Do You see that it is lunch time? Do You see that I am trying to honor one of Your saints? Do You see my hurt? Do You know how much an engine repair costs? Do You know how long it takes to repair an engine even if a repair shop had an engine in stock? Do You see me, Lord? Are you there?

I remind myself that God does care, and He wants me to give Him my cares. Forgive me, Lord, for questioning Your care and Your knowledge of my situation. Lord, I know this isn't about me. Forgive me for my pride. I need Your grace just to think right. I need Your grace just to be able to say thank you in this situation.

12:00 p.m.

"Where are you headed?" the car carrier driver asks us. "Well, we are trying to get to Cedar City where we could stay with friends while we get the van diagnosed," Steve informs the driver. "Hmmm," responds the driver. The silence was deafening. None of us were prepared for what he said. "Well, I could get you to Cedar City by loading the van on my car carrier." Whoa!

God, You do know my situation; and You do see my hurt; and You do have a solution that is so much more creative and more productive than I could ever have expected. Thank you, Lord, for blessing me even when my faith was lacking.

Not long after the driver offered us a ride, AAA comes pulling up to tow us to Cedar City. Steve explains the situation to them, they take down our information, and they drive away. As the driver is preparing to drive the van onto the car carrier, he asks us where we were headed before we broke down. We share with him the death of our grandpa and how we were in the middle of vacation but are now headed back home to attend a funeral. "Where's home?" the driver asks. "We live about two hours southeast of Las Vegas," I answer. The driver pauses briefly, "Well, you know, my route takes me to Vegas tonight; and I could take you all the way if you wanted me to do that."

I cannot explain in words just how the truck driver's words sank deeply into my soul—all of our souls, as we stood there in complete amazement of God's provision and care for us. Esther, my sister-in-law, begins to cry. The joy and relief were too much to hold in. I found myself taking a short stroll in the desert to ponder just how much I was foolish at doubting God. I then laugh through my tears and look to heaven, wondering if Grandpa is smiling down on our situation. I found comfort in being amused at our experiences and God's solutions knowing that Grandpa would have loved to hear the story, only now he got to witness the whole event from above. Tears of joy flowed freely at the thought.

Our angel driver, as we began to call him, loaded the van (with five of us in the van on the top deck of the carrier), and headed to Cedar City. While at Cedar City, he graciously stopped for a food and bathroom break. While in Cedar City, I asked him more questions about his own life and family. He shared with us that he is an LDS (Mormon) who used to live in California but moved to Salt Lake for a better life. Esther and I conclude that most likely there is no such thing as a Mormon angel from heaven, but we remained thankful for this man's generosity and service.

Lord, thank you for allowing us to break down so we could be reminded of Your amazing care and protection. Maybe we broke down just so You could remind me that You are dependable; I don't know. What I do know is that You are the God of peace and safety. Thank you for both.

6:00 p.m.
We arrive in Las Vegas, and our driver takes us all the way to the auto shop of our choice where our friends were waiting for us with our Suburban. We did a quick switch of our luggage, and we were back on the road within a half hour. We tried to hand our angel driver gas money, but he refused. He just wanted to do some good, he says.

9:00 p.m.
We arrive home—just four hours past our expected arrival. We saved

115

in gas money. We have a story to tell. We saw prayers answered within minutes of praying them. A day later we were told the van didn't have a blown engine and was worth getting repaired. (The van was fixed and ready for Daniel and his family to drive home later that week.) Most importantly, I was reminded that God knows and handles the details in my life. I don't understand the peace He gives me, but I can speak of its reality. I don't understand His ways, but I can speak of His care and good will.

In the end, I rediscovered God's provision in a way that seems almost too bizarre to be true. I found through this experience so many reasons to know, trust, and obey God more. If we would have driven from Denver to California with no break downs and no safety hazards, we would have paused to say thank you to God for taking care of us. The prayer would have been sincere, but a certain freshness would be missing. I believe that God desires for us to be "shook up" from time to time to bring back some freshness and luster in our faith. I know myself enough to realize that God sent this event into my life at the very moment when I needed to ponder God more than anything or anyone else in my life.

Lord, I came to You asking You to care for my grandpa while I was away on vacation. You did just that by taking him home to safety and perfect health. I came to You asking You to give us safety on the road. You did just that in a way that only You could orchestrate. My thoughts and my hopes are in You. I have peace.

Tuesday, August 15, 2006
The next forty-eight hours were sweet and sad all at once. Surrounded by family and friends, I rested in the sweet memories of an amazing grandfather; sustained by the promises of God, I rested in the hope that God's ways are best. I talked to God often about how I felt and how I hurt. I thanked God many times for His care and goodness. I thought constantly on the Philippians 4 mandate, and I learned much about God. I found myself being motivated to emulate my grandpa's faithful Christian walk.

Jim Berg, author of *Taking Time to Quiet Your Soul*, exhorts us to be careful about our thoughts and actions even in the midst of sorrow. "Watch how you muse and what you choose when you lose."[1] In God's time, He will deliver us from the sorrow that we feel over the loss of a loved one. Learning to follow "The Philippian Path to Peace" is just one way that we begin to value what God values even in the midst of sadness. The death of a saint is a beautiful thing in God's eyes. Instead of Grandpa saying, "God is with me," God is now saying, "Your grandpa is with Me." Praise the Lord! I would not want my grandpa to be any other place than in God's presence.

God's Hospitality

Wouldn't it be amazing if the White House chief of staff called us today and invited us to attend a special dinner with the President of the United States, and we were the guest of honor? I would immediately begin to pick out my best outfit, make sure my hair was styled correctly, review the rules of table etiquette, rehearse and possibly even write down all of the statements and questions I have for the President, research the President's background so that I would be prepared to carry on meaningful conversation, and arrive thirty minutes early to guarantee I would not be late. An invitation from the President is special. But let us think for a moment if the White House chief of staff called us and said that the President is planning to spend some time in *our* home. There would still be a flurry of dress checks, hair styling, rule reviewing, rehearsing, and researching that would go on; but the honor would be even greater to have the President come to *our* home and be a part of *our* world. The anticipation would be tremendous.

When I received Christ as my Savior, I invited God to take residence in my life. Out of His love for me, He found joy in coming to my home and being a guest in my life for the duration of my life, just as I would find joy in being the President's guest at a special dinner. As my earthly death nears, I truly believe that the Lord treasures the thought of finally having me in *His* home and in *His* domain, just as I would anticipate having the President in my home. For so long the Lord has taken residence in my home, and He yearns for the opportunity to show me the pleasures He has arranged for me forevermore.

There is a unique difference between going to someone's home for a special event and having the special event in our own home. Both are special, but the latter carries with it more thought, more preparation, more anticipation, and more opportunities to share with others our home, our surroundings, our memories. God anticipates my coming to His home. John 14 records that God is preparing for my coming to *His* home. I cannot wait for Him to share with *me His* home.

The Treasured Soul

David writes in Psalm 139:17-18, "How precious also are thy thoughts unto me, O God! how great is the sum of them! If I should count them, they are more in number than the sand: when I awake, I am still with thee." When I read Psalm 139, I read of a Creator Who is intrinsically involved in my life from start to finish—everywhere I go, everything I do, and everything I am. Not only is God involved in my life, He also thinks about me so much that those thoughts cannot be numbered. David calls those thoughts of God precious. Other passages sum up David's awe of God's thoughts toward us.

Job 7:17—What is man, that thou shouldest magnify him? and that thou shouldest set thine heart upon him?

Psalm 8:4—What is man, that thou art mindful of him? and the son of man, that thou visitest him?

Psalm 144:3—LORD, what is man, that thou takest knowledge of him! or the son of man, that thou makest account of him!

Who are we that God should think on us? Who are we that God should set His heart on us? Who are we that God should expend so much energy on us? Who are we that God visits us and takes pleasure in being with us? Who are we that God takes the time to know us?

God knows his people with a tender intimacy, a constant, careful observation: he foreknew them in love, he knows them by care, he will know them in acceptance at last. Why and wherefore is this? What has man done? What has he been? What is he now that God should know him, and make himself known to him as his goodness, fortress, and high tower? This is an unanswerable question. Infinite condescension can alone account for the Lord stooping to be the friend of man. That he should make man the subject of election, the object of redemption, the child of eternal love, the darling of infallible providence, the next of kin to Deity, is indeed a matter requiring more than the two notes of exclamation found in this verse.[2]

The same God Who is mindful of me on earth is the same God Who is preparing for my entrance into heaven. Who am I that God would prepare for me a mansion? Who am I that God would treasure my coming to heaven? Who am I? The answer lies in answering "Who is God?" I am nothing, but because God is everything, His love, grace, and mercy abound beyond my understanding. God treasures my soul. My homecoming is precious to Him. He knows the date of my heavenly entrance, and He stands ready for me with open arms.

Valuing the Death of a Saint
If I am to value what God values, how do I value the death of saints? The following list is a simple but practical way we can value what God values.

1. **Mourn the loss with perspective.** Each culture has different ways of mourning. In the Bible alone we read of people who wept loudly, beat their body, wore sackcloth and ashes, fasted, cut themselves, rent clothes, wore black, hired women to mourn and scream for them, hosted a mourning feast, lay down in silence, covered their head and face, walked barefoot, and removed jewelry. The grief was displayed for all to see. In today's western culture, grief is more private than the eastern cultures. The amount of crying or intensity of weeping a person does or does not do is hardly a measurable way to determine the extent of his mourning. The Bible does not tell us to all mourn the same way. God does remind us that joy will come, and He does want us to grieve with hope.

   Acts 24:15—And have hope toward God, which they themselves also allow, that there shall be a resurrection of the dead, both of the just and unjust.

Psalm 42:11—Why art thou cast down, O my soul? and why art thou disquieted within me? hope thou in God: for I shall yet praise him, who is the health of my countenance, and my God.

2. **Remember life is but a vapor.** I am sure that everyone reading this book has been touched by death, whether the loss was a family member, close friend, or church member. Each and every time we sit in a funeral or memorial service, we need to remind ourselves that life is short and fleeting. God does not promise our next breath, but He does promise eternal life to all who will believe. We need to honor men and women who lived life fully and faithfully for the Lord. Because God determines our homecoming, I need to realize that my son or husband is just as safe in a war as he is playing or working in our backyard. Death will only come if God allows it. Until that day does come, I need to be mindful to live life fully and faithfully today for God. We cannot die right if we have not lived right.

3. **Proclaim the gospel.** We need to view the death of saints as opportunities to proclaim the gospel, for it is the gospel that made possible their sainthood, and it is the gospel that will transform souls so they, too, can have the confidence of eternal life. We can value death by speaking of the truths that keep us from eternal death, which is separation from God.

4. **Accept changes.** One of the hardest things about death is change. Death catapults change. Sometimes death means a change in locations, finances, daily routines, relationships, dependencies, staffing, and neighbors. None of this comes easily. I have caught myself several times beginning to walk over to my grandpa's home to tell him about my day, only to remember he is not there and that I have new neighbors. We develop companionships, and death changes those daily routines and relationships. I wanted to fight those changes at first, but I had to keep remembering that God orchestrated my grandpa's homecoming. If I believe that Grandpa died at the precise time God meant for him to die, then I have to also believe that God meant for me to live and learn from the changes that my grandpa's death brings to me. Why fight them? Why stay sad over the changes? Are the changes hard? Yes. Do the changes hurt? Yes. Do I

mourn those changes? No. I mourn the earthly loss of companionship, but I do not grieve over the changes, because those changes are initiated by God Who knows and does what is good in my life. (By the way, my new neighbors are gracious people. I am thankful.)

5. **Comfort each other.** After the loss of my grandparents, my local church was and continues to be a beacon of comfort and aid to my family. They did the big and little things: supplied food, provided music at the services, prayed, cleaned, made phone calls, oversaw burial services, babysat, printed memorial programs, and did more praying. Through their compassionate care, they comforted us. They came alongside us and hurt with us but also rejoiced with us. They came home after a busy day and cooked for thirty or more people. They took time out of a busy schedule to attend a memorial service to honor a faithful church member. They told us they were praying for us. They hugged us and shook our hands and put an arm around our shoulders. They helped move furniture. They purchased refreshments and tissues and flowers. And the list could go on and on. I needed my local church family more than I thought I needed them. Through death, our church united, served each other, and grew spiritually. No wonder God values the death of saints—He sees how death can help church families come together.

The command to comfort is an important one. We need to show our brothers and sisters in Christ that we care for them, hurt with them, and rejoice with them. I have heard it said that weddings are good to attend in order to show support to the new couple, but that funerals are so much more important and more needful to attend in order to encourage and comfort a grieving family while honoring the one who has died. From experience, I wholeheartedly agree with this statement.

I am sure there are even more ways we can value the death of a saint. My prayer is that whether I am touched by death or whether I have the opportunity to comfort a fellow brother or sister in Christ, I will respond in such a way that I clearly value what God values. By remembering that God values the death (homecoming) of His saints, we can better face the hardships and grief that death brings to those that are left on earth. Yes, God is with me right now, but someday I will get to be *with God* in His home. I can't wait!

Nearer Home

One sweetly solemn thought
Comes to me o'er and o'er;
I'm nearer my home today
Than I ever have been before;

Nearer my Father's house,
Where the many mansions be;
Nearer the great white throne,
Nearer the crystal sea.

Nearer the bound of life,
Where we lay our burdens down;
Nearer leaving the cross,
Nearer gaining the crown!

But lying darkly between,
Winding down through the night,
Is the silent, unknown stream,
That leads at last to the light.

Oh, if my mortal feet
Have almost gained the brink;
If it be I am nearer home
Even today than I think——

Father, perfect my trust!
Let my spirit feel, in death,
That her feet are firmly set
On the Rock of a living faith!

--Phoebe Cary[3]

THE WORTH OF THIS TREASURE

Psalm 116:15

Precious in the sight of the LORD is the death of his saints.

- Its Origin: Everyone will die, but not everyone is a saint. A person becomes a saint at salvation.
- Its Purpose: God's way of bringing me home to heaven and reminding those on earth that life is just a vapor
- Its Potential: Heaven; eternal rest; earthly comfort

What keeps me from valuing the death of a saint? Sorrowing without hope; improper thinking.

A Meek and Quiet Spirit

8

1 Peter 3:4

But let it be the hidden man of the heart, in that which is not corruptible, even the ornament of a meek and quiet spirit, which is in the sight of God of great price.

My dad is an amazing father. I have not always been appreciative of his fatherly ways, but I have learned over the years to value them and learn from them. I sincerely believe that everything my dad did for us and with us was for a purpose. He is not a man of many words; but when he did speak, we learned to listen.

Some of those "fatherly ways" stick out in my mind more than others. This one such "fatherly way" occurred when I was in high school. By this time in my life, I thought I had the answers. I was often cocky, sarcastic, and judgmental. But I will never forget the way my dad handled my poor response on one particular night. It was not the first time I had responded quickly and abruptly, but it was the first time I realized I had a problem and needed to change. My dad's approach to my uncomely speech got my attention.

I remember that all of my family members were sitting around the table. We were nearing the end of dinner; and as was common in our household, we finished our meal and sat around chewing the rest of the ice in our glasses while discussing some issue or event. I made a comment about a family member, and my comment was not funny, although I chuckled at what I said. I did not really notice (until moments later) that the rest of the family just stared at me. The comment was not helpful, but I thought truth was important to share. (I often justified my sarcasm by saying I needed to tell the truth.) I remember vividly my dad's body language after I sarcastically spued criticism toward a family member. All of my family seemed to freeze. Chewing ice is not a quiet activity, and it became obvious that my dad had stopped chewing his ice. I then knew my comment had not gone over very well. I, too, seemed to freeze. We were all waiting for Dad's cue to begin moving again. I was hoping I would get a good laugh from at least one of my brothers, but I did not. Instead, I remember my dad poignantly saying my name, "Shannon." He then sighed, slowly turned his head to me (I sat to his left), and finished his sentence while looking directly at me. "Sometimes you have no tact." All of a sudden, I felt all of my family's eyes on me. I saw the sadness in my dad's eyes. I quickly turned away from his gaze. I immediately wished I could leave the table.

My memory of that evening stops with that comment and the feeling of embarrassment and shame. I have no idea what else was said or how the evening ended. What I do remember is that my dad got my attention. He said very little, but the words he did say burned within my heart. I realized I had hurt my dad. I had disappointed him. The truth I felt so necessary to say lacked both love and mercy.

"Shannon, sometimes you have no tact" is a reminder to me that I constantly need to guard my mouth and keep a door on my lips. My dad's quiet but firm way of getting my attention was very effective. I must confess: I still struggle with sarcasm and overdone satire. I am still not the most tactful lady in the room, but that night so long ago made me aware of my problem and my need to depend on God's grace to help me control my tongue.

When I read 1 Peter 3:4 and the importance God places on a woman's spiritual adornment, I remember my dad's statement: "Shannon, sometimes you have no tact." I praise the Lord for how far He has brought me, but I pray for help with the rest of the mountain climb.

The Context of 1 Peter 3

God tells us in 1 Peter 3 that God considers a meek and quiet spirit in a woman to be precious. Not only are these qualities priceless, but they also are incorruptible (without decay). The meek and quiet treasure reminds us of the Matthew 6:20 description of God's treasures: they will not rust or be destroyed. They truly are incorruptible.

1 Peter 3:4 falls in the middle of a list of verses about the opportunities a woman has when she responds correctly to her husband (verses 2 and 5), when she lives modestly (verses 1-2), when she cultivates a God-pleasing inward character (verses 3-4), and when she trusts in the Lord (verse 5). The meek and quiet spirit is at the center of these opportunities.

Before we delve any deeper into this subject, we need to recall again the lessons we learned from studying God's lovingkindness. How does God draw us to Him? In essence, how did He win us and how does He continue to draw us to Him? God, by the Holy Spirit, does so through His goodness. Peter parallels this same principle but applies it to wives. According to 1 Peter 3, we win our husbands by how we behave and respond to them. We do not win them with harsh words or with Bible-thumping speeches. "The way God takes to overcome evil in us is, under our provocations, to heap goodness on us. If a Christian wife would conquer her unbelieving husband for Christ, she must in this imitate the Divine procedure."[1] In the same way some people will reject God despite His constant goodness, some husbands will reject God despite a wife's meekness and quietness, but the principle is still effective and commanded in this passage. Whether a husband is believing, unbelieving, backslidden, lukewarm, in full-time ministry, or a baby Christian, our responsibility *and* privilege as a wife is to submit in the same manner as we would submit to God's authority in our lives.

Paul writes in Ephesians 5:22, "Wives, submit yourselves unto your own husbands, as unto the Lord." What does it mean to submit to our husbands as unto the Lord? I covered this topic of submission in my ladies' Sunday school class, and I was a little fearful of teaching on submission. I did not feel adequate or experienced enough to teach it. But by listing six specific ways we are commanded to submit to God, I found applying submission to be less complex than I thought. I learned much from this study. For further details on submitting as unto the Lord, I have included passages and parallels (Appendix E) that helped me better understand my roles as a wife to my husband and as a child to my Lord. Below are listed those six areas of how wives should submit to God and their husbands. This list is not exhaustive, but it gives us a starting point.

- With full faith
- With joy
- With knowledge
- With reverence
- With love
- With thankfulness

We cannot study the importance of our inner character as found in 1 Peter 3:4 without covering the joy of submission found in verses 1 and 2 and verses 5 and 6. Verses 3 and 4 are sandwiched between verses 1 and 2 and 5 and 6. Just as a hamburger would be quite bland and not really a hamburger at all without the juicy meat inside, so our lives would be quite bland and really hypocritical if we failed to cultivate the important center of us—our hearts.

The outer part of the sandwich helps bring out the flavor of the inside meat. My outward actions—specifically how I obey and live—bring out the real me inside. Back in the 80s, the fast-food chain restaurant Wendy's began advertising beefier hamburgers and came out with a commercial where three old ladies go through a drive-thru at a competing hamburger joint. After they receive their burgers, all three ladies take a bite. As soon as they bite into the burger, the old ladies stare into the wrapper and then loudly ask, "Where's the beef?" For years the slogan "Where's the beef?" was used to remind folks that Wendy's had more meat in their hamburgers than their competing fast-food restaurants. When our husbands spend time with us, do they walk away asking, "Where's her real beauty?" or do they praise the Lord for a woman that is not only actively doing what is right outwardly but is also spending time cultivating her inward heart in order to be beautiful in God's eyes? We cannot fail to invest time and energy in cultivating our heart's adornment. It is the center of our actions and reactions (Matthew 15:19; Mark 7:21). Submission is not what is precious; living a chaste life is not what is precious. Cultivating our inner man—taking time to make sure our spirit is beautiful to God—is what is precious to God.

Adorning the Outward

Let us read again the key verses in this chapter: "Whose adorning let it not be that outward adorning of plaiting the hair, and of wearing of gold, or of putting on of apparel; But let it be the hidden man of the heart, in that which is not corruptible, even the ornament of a meek and quiet spirit, which is in the sight of God of great price" (1 Peter 3:3-4).

I am so glad that the Apostle Peter was not telling me to stop adorning altogether! As I studied this passage, I was surprisingly appreciative of how the commentaries applied verse 3. Here is a spattering of what they said.

That attention to dress and personal decoration is natural to women, is obvious from an observation of the customs of every nation in every age. The Apostle Peter must not be understood as in this place censuring such attention, but as pointing out that there is apparel, that there is ornament, far preferable to any bodily costume and jewelry that wealth can purchase. Christian women of every position in life are exhorted to provide themselves with these precious and incomparable recommendations; to cultivate, above all things, "a meek and quiet spirit."[2]

It is implied here that it is natural for women to love to adorn themselves. A wife who has not some regard for ornament in her house or person, who is plainness, if not a slattern, who has not a flower to delight the eye, is not likely to have much influence with her husband even for Christianity.[3]

... this text doth not absolutely forbid the wearing of ornaments or costly apparel by such persons whose quality will answer it, but only forbids pride and vanity, affectation and ostentation, in the wearing of them; it is not only lawful to cover the body, but to adorn the body; Abraham had never sent ear-rings and bracelets to Rebekah, had they been sinful in their use: to wear such things beyond our purse and place, and to make ourselves or others poor by making ourselves fine, is very sinful, but otherwise, lawful.[4]

Peter did not state that women should not wear jewelry and nice clothes, but that Christian wives should not think of outer attire as the source of genuine beauty.[5]

The general consensus is that Peter, in writing God's inspired words, never forbade women from taking care of their outward body. As a matter of principle, the Bible does tell us to do things decently and in order and that God is not a God of confusion. Our clothing and our outward appearance should send a clear message of wanting to honor God. There are several books about modesty that are worthy of reading. *What Is Modesty?* by Michelle Brock and *Secret Keeper: The Delicate Power of Modesty* by Dannah Gresh are both outstanding in principle and practicality. Modesty does not mean frumpy. We can enjoy adorning ourselves, while remaining modest in our attitude and appearance, when we dress and behave in ways that honor God.

Adorning the Inward

My soul and spirit will live forever. Each year that I celebrate a birthday, I resign to the reality that my skin will not look young forever, my hair will not have the same shine, and my muscles will eventually lose their shape. Peter speaks to our common sense when he says that we should spend time adorning our immortal soul with incorruptible and priceless ornaments. Why spend large amounts of time and money on items that adorn our outward bodies but have no lasting value?

Even the finest of jewelry will lose its shine and brilliance over time, but not the ornaments that Peter speaks of. "But let it be the hidden man of the heart, in that which is not corruptible, even the ornament of a meek and quiet spirit, which is in the sight of God of great price." We read in this verse that a meek and quiet spirit has two benefits: it is incorruptible, and it is precious to God.

A Meek Adornment

A meek spirit can best be described as a mild or gentle spirit. Some may say that being meek is being humble, but meekness is a *fruit* of humility. "It is only the humble heart which is also the meek, and which, as such, does not fight against God and more or less struggle and contend with Him."[6] Being meek is resting in the Lord's ways, because a person with a meek spirit has already determined by faith and through experience that God is always good. Many would describe the events in Moses' life as tragic: people and circumstances did not make his life easy. Yet, Moses was described as a meek man (Numbers 12:3). Resting in God's goodness is recognizing that the good times and bad times are still God-ordained times in my life.

A Quiet Adornment

A quiet spirit can best be described as a tranquil or peaceful spirit. This phrase *quiet spirit* does not imply that women should be silent and never speak. The Greek word actually means "keeping one's seat."[7] How do fans at a basketball or football game react when they disagree with a referee's call? They stand up in protest! Rarely do we see avid fans sitting down during the tense moments of a sporting event. A woman with a quiet spirit does not get riled during tense moments in life. What would be a tense moment in life? My baby is crying, dinner is cooking and beginning to burn, another child is calling for more toilet paper, my husband is walking through the door from a long day of work, the dog is chewing on a baby toy, and the phone is ringing . . . again. How would we respond to this tense moment? We have two choices: scream and shove a few problems to our husband, or greet our husband and begin dealing with each emergency one at a time. I would hope none of us would think that the phone needed to be answered at that moment!

We need to take some time to evaluate what makes us "rise from our seats" in protest. How do we respond to injustices, flat tires, tight budgets, forgotten dates, rumors, temptations, tense moments, weariness, busy schedules, no romance, another errand, hurtful words, anger, broken appliances, carpool problems, school troubles, church responsibilities, a disastrous dinner meal, and no communication? Do we respond with flare-ups, or have we prior to the tense moment, concluded that God is allowing the moment to occur and that He always has our good in mind? If we have not solidified this core belief—that God has allowed the event or person to enter my life and that He has my good in mind—then we will struggle with having a meek and quiet spirit. We will rise from our seats in protest to God, and everyone around us will wish they were sitting in a different part of the bleachers.

We cannot turn on a meek and quiet spirit like a light switch, for a meek and quiet spirit occurs when a person knows, trusts, and obeys God. And here we visit our KTO process again . . . the more I know God, the more I will trust Him; the more I trust God, the more I discover that He is faithful; the more I see of God's faithfulness, the more I find that obeying Him brings joy and contentment, so much so that I want to get to know Him more. I cannot be meek without knowing and firmly believing that God is the source of my power. I cannot be quiet without knowing and firmly believing that God is in control of my life. I cannot be meek or quiet without knowing and firmly believing that without God's help, I can be neither. Meekness knowingly, not blindly, depends on a powerful God; and quietness actively puts that belief into practice by responding righteously to what God brings to the playing field.

How can I respond righteously to the pressures of life? In Luke 6:46-49, Jesus describes two different houses that faced the same storm. The houses' foundations were not the same—one was rock and one was sand—and this made all the difference in how they handled the storms. In the same way that a house's foundation determines how it will stand up against a storm, so a Christian's foundation—one built upon God's Word, or one built upon man's reasoning—will determine how he stands against life's pressures.

Poor Responses to Pressures	Righteous Responses to Pressures
Fear	Faith in promises
Depression	Joy in the trial; hope in God's solutions
Anger	Peace that passes all understanding
Panic	Quiet assurance in God's sovereignty
Guilt	Ready to forgive; humbled by forgiveness
Burnout	Endurance through God's strength
Quitting	Dependence on God
Selfishness	Sacrificial love to others; serving others
Bitterness	Forgiveness

As a Christian, God is my ultimate referee. He makes the calls. I could rise in protest to those calls, but the response would be futile, if not sinful. Not only is God my ultimate referee, but He also places other referees in my life. These other referees are the authorities in my life: my husband, pastor, parents, teachers, employer, and government officials. They make calls in my life, too. Those referees are in my life because God has placed them in my life, and my job is to "keep my seat" and respond righteously to their calls. The question is whether I will be grounded in the truths of God's Word in order to respond properly.

We do not have to go through hard times in order to have a meek and quiet spirit. Our responses to pressures are indications of our heart's foundation. God often uses circumstances to show us where we need to change in order to become more like Him. Romans 5:1-5 outlines for us the way God uses circumstances to draw us closer to Him as we respond correctly to His refereeing in our lives.

Therefore being justified by faith,

We have been saved by faith.

we have peace with God through our Lord Jesus Christ:

Peace means "to join"; to have quietness and rest. My relationship with Christ (my joining with Him) begins at salvation.

By whom also we have access by faith into this grace wherein we stand,

Our faith at salvation gives us immediate favor with God. I can boldly go to God.

and rejoice in hope of the glory of God.

I have happiness in looking forward to God's eternal glory.

And not only so,

There's more . . .

but we glory in tribulations also:

We can rejoice in various trials that we have to endure on earth (such as troubles and injustices that make me want to protest God's call). We can rejoice because of our salvation and because of our trials.

knowing

I base my rejoicing not on feelings, but on a knowledge.

that tribulation worketh

I know that my trials will produce something; my trials will prove something, and by proving, I will improve.

patience;

My trials will produce endurance, which is the ability to bear suffering with calmness and unwavering fortitude—a quiet attitude.

And patience, experience;

My trials will bear proof that God is faithful—a meek response.

and experience, hope:

My trials will give me a confident expectation, which is the sustaining of my soul, that will allow me to patiently anticipate what comes next for God's glory.

And hope maketh not ashamed;

My hope will not cause me to blush or be shamed or disgraced. I am confident.

because the love of God is shed abroad in our hearts

I am confident because God's love spills out and pours forth as I continue to hope and bear proof of God's faithfulness in sustaining me.

by the Holy Ghost which is given unto us.
We bear witness of these truths through the Holy Spirit that resides in us.

When I follow the progression of Romans 5, and I apply these verses directly to my life, I begin to adorn my immortal soul with an incorruptible and precious treasure called a meek and quiet spirit. Despite the pressures in life, I can be meek and quiet in my responses.

Obtaining and Treasuring the Inward Ornaments

Obtaining a meek and quiet spirit requires us to go back to the core truths of God's Word. The "must-believe truths" found in chapter 4 of this book are the key ingredients to building a strong foundation and are vital to my having a meek and quiet spirit.

Let us revisit these must-believe truths that should be a part of our foundation.

I must believe that God is holy and that I am in need of His holiness.

- Isaiah 57:15
- 1 Samuel 2:2-3
- Is there anything in my life that shows that I do not believe God is holy and that I do not need to be like Him?

I must believe that God is love and that I am in need of His love.

- Jeremiah 31:3
- Ephesians 2:4-5
- Is there anything in my life that shows that I do not believe God loves me and that I need to love others?

I must believe that God is right and that I am in need of His righteousness and instruction in righteousness.

- Ezra 9:15
- Hosea 14:9
- 2 Timothy 3:16-17
- Is there anything in my life that shows that I do not believe that God is right and that I need to rest in His justice?

I must believe that God is just and that I am in need of His mercy.

- Micah 7:9
- Ecclesiastes 12:14
- Is there anything in my life that shows that I do not believe that God is merciful and that I need to extend mercy to others?

I must believe that God is powerful and that I am in need of His protection.

- Ephesians 1:19-20
- Matthew 19:24-26
- Is there anything in my life that shows that I do not believe that God is powerful enough to help me and that I am trying to do everything on my own?

I must believe that God is kind and that I am in need of His care.

- Titus 3:4-7
- Psalm 36:7-8
- 1 Peter 5:7
- Is there anything in my life that shows that I do not believe that God is always kind and that I need to depend on that kindness to take care of me?

I must believe that God is for me and that I am in need of His grace.

- Psalm 86:5
- Nahum 1:7
- Psalm 139:17-18
- Is there anything in my life that shows that I do not believe that God is on my side and therefore am proudly standing up for my rights?

I must believe that God is faithful and that I can trust Him.

- Lamentations 3:22-23
- Deuteronomy 7:8-10
- 1 Corinthians 10:13

- Is there anything in my life that shows that I do not believe in God's faithfulness and that I do not trust Him to sustain me?

Believing these truths changes our inner spirit causing our outward responses to be biblical. Having a knowledge of these truths is not enough; we need to believe them. Evaluating our responses and behaviors is important as we desire to adorn our hearts with God's treasures.

Making the Gospel Sparkle

Just as I believe that God considers marriage to be precious because it is a representation of the relationship between Christ and the church, I also believe that God considers a meek and quiet spirit precious to Him because it promotes the gospel message to our loved ones. The context of 1 Peter 3 really does give us a glimpse into God's heart. Yes, a meek and quiet spirit makes a woman beautiful inside, but this inner beauty itself is not what is precious to God. A meek and quiet spirit will also make a woman easier to live with; however, living peaceably with others is not why God considers a meek and quiet spirit precious. I believe that God considers a meek and quiet spirit valuable because this inward adorning of our heart produces godly behavior that wins the lost for Christ. One author summarizes the importance of a woman's godly behavior:

> This must be the aspiration of all mothers and daughters: the successful transfer of the qualities of biblical womanhood that sparkle with the gospel—so that in the midst of this me-centered, self-focused, ungodly language of our culture, we can speak the refreshingly pure, altogether true, and saving message of Jesus Christ.[8]

Our behavior and our responses, which are a direct outflow of our inward man, can and should make the gospel sparkle so that others will see God through us. A meek and quiet spirit will exemplify the gospel, and that kind of spirit is precious to God and should be valued by us. If we treasure the gospel like we should, we will do all we can to make the gospel sparkle and come alive for others to see. The opposite of meekness and quietness is self-centered living. Treasuring meekness and quietness is gospel-centered living.

THE WORTH OF THIS TREASURE

1 Peter 3:4

But let it be the hidden man of the heart, in that which is not corruptible, even the ornament of a meek and quiet spirit, which is in the sight of God of great price.

- Its Origin: Found in the inner man when I emulate Christ and His Word
- Its Purpose: To draw others to Christ; to make the gospel sparkle
- Its Potential: Improved relationship with husband; incorruptible beauty

What keeps me from valuing a meek and quiet spirit? Unbelief; pride; misaligned priorities; selfishness.

Wisdom 9

Proverbs 3:13-15

Happy is the man that findeth wisdom, and the man that getteth understanding. For the merchandise of it is better than the merchandise of silver, and the gain thereof than fine gold. She is more precious than rubies: and all the things thou canst desire are not to be compared unto her.

Benjamin Franklin was right when he said, "Many foxes grow gray, but few grow good."[1] If turning gray meant that we would be wiser and better, our world would be showing vast improvements, especially since many nations have seen an increase in the population of the elderly. People are living longer. Age seventy is no longer the average life expectancy age; as a matter of fact, seventy will most likely become the new retirement age. The world is getting older, but it does not appear to be getting any wiser. "Great men are not always wise: neither do the aged understand judgment" (Job 32:9).

If I thought the gray that is persistently showing up in my hair brought automatic wisdom, I would welcome each straight, stiff hair, despite its rebellion to any curlers or softeners. I would not resist the culture of our day that says gray-haired men look distinguished and gray-haired women just look old. Common sense and observation tell me that gray hair is not necessarily a sign of wisdom; it is just a sign of experience. Although experience is a great teacher, I find that many of us are lousy learners.

Lessons from Job

Job's life is epic. Anyone who believes that the Bible imitates literature has forgotten that the book of Job is probably the oldest recorded story. Job's life story has all of the important literature elements that make a good story. By literary standards, the book of Job is an excellent biography. We have the initial setting where we are introduced to a character who has a great life. The rising action of conflict begins when we get to overhear a conversation between Satan and God. Before long, we cannot put the book down because we want to find out what Satan is going to do to Job. We learn quite early in the story of Satan's horrific plans for Job, which God allowed him to accomplish—to destroy his wealth, family, and health. But the story does not end there. The plot only thickens as we are introduced to Job's friends who begin to discourse their supposed causes for Job's hardships. The conflict rises and falls throughout these discourses as Job defends his honor and his God in the midst of horrible, often depressing, advice from his friends. The climax of the story comes when God addresses Job and challenges his ignorance: "Gird up now thy loins like a man; for I will demand of thee, and answer thou me" (38:3). It is as if God pulled Job up out of the ashes of despondency to question Job about His knowledge and power. The story begins to come together for the reader as Job responds to God's challenge by saying, "Behold, I am vile; what shall I answer thee? I will lay mine hand upon my mouth" (40:4). God continues to speak as Job silently listens and learns. At the conclusion of God's challenge, Job submits to God, "I know that thou canst do everything, and that no thought can be withholden from thee . . . I have heard of thee by the hearing of the ear; but now mine eye seeth thee: wherefore I abhor myself, and repent in dust and ashes" (42:2, 5-6). The story's resolution is Job's submission and God's abundant forgiveness and blessing.

Job's story has deep characters, bad guys and good guys, tragedy, relationships, and a happy ending. I can imagine that many children of Israel begged moms and dads to tell the story of Job as a bedtime story.

Throughout the book of Job, we are able to read Job's very thoughts, struggles, and beliefs. In chapter 28, Job compares finding wisdom to a miner who searches for treasure. In the midst of tragedy, poor advice, and little-to-no comfort from friends or family, Job speaks of the importance of finding wisdom. Although now in poverty after Satan's attack, Job saw wisdom as a precious commodity. Job describes a miner who searches the earth, turns over stones, follows paths unknown to animals, and dams up rivers in order to find "every precious thing" that is hidden (28:1-11). This prospector will go to great lengths to find treasure. Job says this miner even "overturneth the mountains by the roots" (verse 9). When we read these verses, we do not picture a lazy miner who may or may not find buried treasure. We see a miner who is engineering, excavating, mapping, damming, and discovering new avenues for mining. He is focused, determined, and passionate about finding precious things under the ground.

Then Job asks this question, "But where shall wisdom be found? And where is the place of understanding? Man knoweth not the price thereof; neither is it found in the land of the living" (verses 12-13). As good as the miner is, he will not find precious wisdom in the earth. No matter how diligent, how creative, how thorough his search may be, every place he looks on earth for wisdom will be the wrong place.

> Job 28:15-19—[Wisdom] cannot be gotten for gold, neither shall silver be weighed for the price thereof. It cannot be valued with the gold of Ophir, with the precious onyx, or the sapphire. The gold and the crystal cannot equal it: and the exchange of it shall not be for jewels of fine gold. No mention shall be made of coral, or of pearls: for the price of wisdom is above rubies. The topaz of Ethiopia shall not equal it, neither shall it be valued with pure gold.

If wisdom is this valuable and if the best of miners cannot find it on earth, the logical question is, "Whence then cometh wisdom? And where is the place of understanding? seeing it is hid from the eyes of all living, and kept close from the fowls of the air?" (verses 20-21)

Then Job states the answer to his own question:

> God understandeth the way thereof, and he knoweth the place thereof. For he looketh to the ends of the earth, and seeth under the whole heaven; To make the weight for the winds; and he weigheth the waters by measure. When he made a decree for the rain, and a way for the lightning of the thunder: Then did he see it, and declare it; he prepared it, yea, and searched it out. And unto man he said, **Behold, the fear of the Lord, that is wisdom; and to depart from evil is understanding** (Job 28:23-28).

Not-So-Buried Treasure

We may wonder at times whether God is playing a hide-and-seek game with wisdom and if we are the pawns in search of finding wisdom in His perfect hiding spot. Proverbs 8 tells us a different story.

- Verse 1:"Doth not wisdom cry?"
  - Verse 2:"[Wisdom] standeth in the top of high places . . . "
  - Verse 3:"[Wisdom] crieth at the gates, at the entry of the city, at the coming in at the doors."
- Verse 4:Wisdom says, "Unto you, O men, I call . . . "
- Verse 5:"Hear," says wisdom, "for I will speak . . . "
- Verse 7:"[Wisdom's] mouth shall speak truth . . . "
  - Verse 9:"[Wisdom's words] are plain to him that understandeth, and right to them that find knowledge."

God wants us to find wisdom, and wisdom wants to be found. We are not talking about buried treasure, but we are talking about a priceless treasure that we would be foolish to ignore. "For wisdom is better than rubies; and all the things that may be desired are not to be compared to it" (Proverbs 8:10-11). God tells us that if we seek wisdom, we will find it. That is a promise we cannot afford to throw away. Proverbs 2 tells us how to seek in order to find wisdom; for although God is the source of wisdom, we must do our part to acquire it.

> Proverbs 2:1-6—My son, if thou wilt **receive my words**, and **hide my commandments** with thee; So that thou **incline thine ear** unto wisdom, and **apply thine heart** to understanding; Yea, if thou **criest after knowledge**, and **liftest up thy voice** for understanding; If thou **seekest her** as silver, and **searchest for her** as for hid treasures; Then shalt thou understand the fear of the LORD, and find the knowledge of God. For the LORD giveth wisdom: out of his mouth cometh knowledge and understanding.

When we separate and define each phrase of Proverbs 2, we discover not a hide-and-seek pattern but rather a seek-and-find pattern.

The Phrase	The Definition
If . . . we receive words	To fetch, to accept, to seize
If . . . we hide commandments	To secretly hoard, to esteem, to protect
If . . . we incline our ears	To prick up the ears, to attend to
If . . . we apply our heart	To cause to yield
If . . . we cry after knowledge	To pronounce, to publish, to invite by name
If . . . we lift up our voice	To shoot forth, to give, to lend
If . . . we seek as for silver	To search, to beseech, to procure something valuable
If . . . we search as for hid treasure	To diligently seek in order to uncover
Then . . . we will understand	To mentally separate truth from error
Then . . . we will find	To attain, to acquire

For God gives wisdom and from His mouth comes knowledge and understanding

Two Kinds of Wisdom

I enjoy reading definitions from America's first dictionary, *Webster's 1828 Dictionary*, because Noah Webster uses examples from the Bible to define words. *Wisdom* is one of those words. According to Webster, wisdom is "true religion; godliness; piety; the knowledge and fear of God, and sincere and uniform obedience to his commands. This is the wisdom which is from above." In defining wisdom, Webster distinguishes between two kinds of wisdom—"the wisdom of this world, mere human erudition; or the carnal policy of men, their craft and artifices in promoting their temporal interests; called also fleshly wisdom."[2] He is referring to the two wisdoms mentioned in James 3.

James 3:13-18—Who is a wise man and endued with knowledge among you? let him shew out of a good conversation his works with meekness of wisdom. But if ye have bitter envying and strife in your hearts, glory not, and lie not against the truth. This wisdom descendeth not from above, but is earthly, sensual, devilish. For where envying and strife is, there is confusion and every evil work. But the wisdom that is from above is first pure, then peaceable, gentle, and easy to be intreated, full of mercy and good fruits, without partiality, and without hypocrisy. And the fruit of righteousness is sown in peace of them that make peace.

Under God's inspiration, James states that earthly wisdom is full of bitter envying and strife, is without truth, and is sensual and devilish. In contrast, wisdom from above is pure, peaceable, gentle, submissive, merciful, full of good works, straightforward, unfeigned, and unwavering. What a difference!

So, the question is, which wisdom do we want? James 1:5 teaches us that when we ask God for wisdom, He is more than willing to give us spiritual wisdom from above. He wants to give us that wisdom liberally, and He does not want to stop giving it to us. Unfortunately, though, I'm afraid that many of us have the worldly view of wisdom in our minds when we ask God for wisdom; and *we expect Him to answer our prayers according to that worldly definition*. We would rather have the prestige of earthly wisdom (despite the fact that earthly wisdom causes confusion and strife). Earthly wisdom is based on man's reasoning; whereas, spiritual wisdom is based on God's holy standard.

Next time we pray for wisdom, we need to keep in mind what the Bible says wisdom is and pray accordingly.

> *Lord, I want to be undefiled; make me pure. I want to be a peacemaker; make me peace-loving. I want to be courteous; make me gentle and considerate. I want to be reasonable; make me submissive. I want to be merciful; give me compassion. I want to produce good fruit; make my motives pure. I want to be honest; make me just and straightforward. I want to be sincere; make my faith strong. I want YOUR wisdom; do all of the above!*

Now that's a fully-loaded prayer. James 1:5-6 puts a condition on those who should ask for wisdom. Only those who lack wisdom need to ask for it. That includes me. Asking for wisdom from above and understanding that it is not earthly wisdom is the first step in treasuring what God treasures! The question remains—do I want it enough to search for it?

The Benefits of Having Wisdom
Investments are often rated based on their returns. If I invest in stocks, and I receive high returns (that is, I receive more than I put in the investment), then my investment is considered sound and successful. If I am hired to buy and sell stocks for clients in order for them to make more money, but I make little-to-no money for my clients, my job is at risk.

Biblical treasures are valued no differently. God is not asking us to invest in treasures that have no earthly or heavenly returns for us. Just as my dad would not ask me to invest in a poorly-run company where I would have to pay in more than I would get back, God, my heavenly Father, is not asking me to spend time pursuing treasures that have no benefit to God or His children. In fact, God *is* saying to invest in these treasures so that we can experience high returns and enormous benefits on earth and in heaven.

Proverbs 3:14 records that wisdom's returns are better than gold: "For the merchandise of it is better than the merchandise of silver, and the gain thereof than fine gold." Gaining wisdom is a trustworthy, low risk, quick return investment that we should grab hold of and not squander.

The Bible tells us in Proverbs 3 that happiness, length of days, pleasantness (being agreeable), peace, riches, and honor are all by-products of possessing God's treasure of wisdom. Those are high returns! We would be foolish to not pursue such a treasure.

We can possess the high returns of wisdom, and we can experience those high returns immediately. Being financially sound is important for every Christian. We should work hard at saving, at investing for our future, at planning ahead, at spending but not overspending, at knowing when to buy and when to sell, and at giving to meet others' needs. Retirement funds are investments we make now so that we can enjoy some security in the years to come. College savings funds are investments we make now so that we can better prepare for our children's higher education. A savings account is an investment we make in order to be ready for unforeseen emergencies or projects. Many of our investments here on earth are for future needs and wants. When we invest in wisdom, we get immediate returns that are for today and last throughout our lifetime.

We do not say to ourselves, "In case I get sad in the future, I'd better pay for some wisdom today so I am prepared." "In case I become disagreeable with my co-worker tomorrow, I'd better buy up some wisdom." "In case I make a mistake in the future and lose my integrity, I'd better save up to buy some wisdom so I can replace my lost honor." Wisdom does not work that way. The Bible clearly says that wisdom cannot be purchased with money or valuables; it can only be found in God. God gives when we search, and we find when we see God. The Bible becomes a valuable tool where we can search and see God.

When we gain wisdom, we immediately begin to experience happiness, pleasantness, and honor, because in our quest for wisdom, we discover Who God is and who we are. When we see God as He really is and we see ourselves as we really are, we find that life is not worth living without God.

The Word of God teaches me that
- I can enjoy today with a security of tomorrow because I discovered in my quest for wisdom that God holds my life in His hands, and in His hands I can rest (Philippians 1:6). Why should I worry?
- I can be pleasant with the unlovable and with the disagreeable because I discovered in my quest for wisdom that God loved me and saved me when I was still a filthy sinner (Ephesians 4:32). Why should I be difficult or expect perfection from others?
- I can be at peace with my circumstances or with those around me because I discovered in my quest for wisdom that God is always good and never makes a mistake. God only allows in my life what is best for me (Romans 8:28-29). Why should I be sad, frustrated, scared, or worried?
- I can be rich with the possessions that I have because I discovered in my quest for wisdom that my possessions are not what makes me wealthy. God, Who owns the cattle on a thousand hills, is the Source

of my wealth (Psalm 84:11). Why should I be discontent with what He gives me or withholds from me?

- I can serve others through my life because I discovered in my quest for wisdom that God gives honor to the humble and to those who do right, and only God's grace enables me to serve the right way. Remembering who I am (nothing without God) and what God did for me (everything that is good in me) results in my desire to honor God through my life (2 Corinthians 12:9). Why then should I hope to gain glory for myself?

So how can we possess this awesome treasure called wisdom? We need to get to know God, to trust Him, to obey Him! One of the first steps to fearing God is knowing God. Do we know Him? Are we seeking a relationship with Him? Are we settling for the world's wisdom when God's wisdom holds so much more for us? "And unto man he said, Behold, the fear of the Lord, that is wisdom; and to depart from evil is understanding" (Job 28:28). The quest for heavenly wisdom is worth every ounce of energy we put into it. The returns cannot be measured. We do not have to wait until we are gray to be wise, nor should we foolishly think that gray hair means we are wise. We do not have to wait until we are retired to cash in on the benefits of having wisdom. We can have wisdom now. This treasure is ours if only we will choose it and seek after it.

THE WORTH OF THIS TREASURE

Proverbs 3:13-15

Happy is the man that findeth wisdom, and the man that getteth understanding. For the merchandise of it is better than the merchandise of silver, and the gain thereof than fine gold. She is more precious than rubies: and all the things thou canst desire are not to be compared unto her.

- Its Origin: From fearing God and by wanting it
- Its Purpose: To be pure, peaceable, gentle, submissive, merciful, full of good works; not wavering
- Its Potential: Happiness; long days; riches; honor; pleasantness; peace

What keeps me from valuing wisdom? Not fearing; not searching; not asking.

The Work
of Christ 10

1 Peter 1:18-19

Forasmuch as ye know that ye were not redeemed with corruptible things, as silver and gold, from your vain conversation received by tradition from your fathers; But with the precious blood of Christ, as of a lamb without blemish and without spot.

The sight of blood is not high on my list of beautiful things. I do not get queasy at the sight of blood like some people do, but I never enjoy seeing it. My sophomore and junior years of high school were filled with ambitions of being a surgeon. Never mind the fact that I did not really enjoy science; I thought being a surgeon would be really cool and prestigious. I most likely saw big houses and fast cars and ignored the long and tedious hours, not to mention the huge school bills that would come with training to be a surgeon. I remember wanting to help people, but I do not believe I was being realistic in my career ambitions during those years.

The turning point in my decision not to be a surgeon happened on a Saturday morning, and I will never forget this life-changing event. My dad decided our family project for the day would be to butcher our chickens! Because we had been a part of the butchering process before (my grandparents owned and operated a turkey ranch), I didn't think much of the chore; my brothers and I actually enjoyed certain moments of the process (not to be discussed in this book for fear of receiving hate mail).

My job in past butchering events at my grandparents' turkey ranch was to catch the poor bird and hand it to my dad or grandpa who then, with the help of my mom and grandma, took care of the rest. Catching chickens was not always easy; so it was not that I had an unimportant job. No chicken in hand, no chicken to butcher. But this Saturday was different. This time my dad graduated me from catching chickens, and my younger brothers were given the chore instead. My promotion was nothing to be proud of because my new job was not very glamorous: I was put in charge of gutting out the freshly killed chickens.

Before long, the entire family had the assembly line working quite efficiently. My younger brothers would catch a chicken, my older brother and dad would chop off the head, my grandparents would dip the dead chicken in hot, boiling water and begin plucking the feathers, and Mom and I would then finish plucking the chicken and gut it out. The job was nasty! Freshly killed chickens do not smell good, and their guts are still warm and very slimy. Eventually, once Mom was confident I knew what I was doing, she moved to the last task of cleaning and packing the chicken for the freezer.

That day I decided that being a surgeon was not what I wanted to do. Because I found no pleasure in cutting open chickens and observing organs, veins, and other grotesque-looking inner parts, I knew I would find no satisfaction in opening up people, no matter how much I wanted to help make them feel better or live longer. My grandfather was quite devastated that I decided I did not want to pursue the medical field. For many months, even years, he reminded me that I once wanted to be a surgeon and that he always wondered why I no longer wanted to pursue it. I am thankful that I now have a cousin that is a pediatrician; so Grandpa was happy to say he had a grandson who is a doctor. I will forever be thankful to my cousin for "distracting" my grandfather so that he did not remind me of my sudden career change.

Even though the sight of blood is not high on my list of beautiful things, Christ's blood is a beautiful treasure. Christ willingly shed *His* own blood for me. His blood, shed for me, is one of God's treasures that does not rust, does not fade, and cannot be stolen. This treasure—the gospel—is the foundation of all other treasures in the Bible.

The Precious Blood of Christ
I find it difficult to comprehend God's love for a people that rejected Him time and time again. Even before He created us, He knew we would sin. In His wisdom and grace, He ordained a plan that would reconcile us sinners to Him without compromising His holiness. And while we were yet sinners, without hope of a future, dead in our sins, and condemned to hell, He sent His Son to die in our place.

> Romans 5:6-8—For when we were yet without strength, in due time Christ died for the ungodly. For scarcely for a righteous man will one

die: yet peradventure for a good man some would even dare to die. But God commendeth his love toward us, in that, while we were yet sinners, Christ died for us.

The *plan* of salvation is not what saves us, though. Salvation became possible when God saw His own Son's blood shed for mankind. Christ's blood was precious in God's sight, paving the way for mankind to be saved from the wrath to come. Christ, the sinless Lamb of Calvary, shed His blood so that we who believe by faith could live forever with God, despite our genes being completely sinful. We Christians are justified by Christ's blood (Romans 5:9). Christ's shedding of His blood is precious in God's sight.

> 1 Peter 1:18-19—Forasmuch as ye know that ye were not redeemed with corruptible things, as silver and gold, from your vain conversation received by tradition from your fathers; But with the precious blood of Christ, as of a lamb without blemish and without spot.

Because God treasures Christ's shed blood, we should treasure it, too. But beyond that assumption, we should treasure Christ's blood because of what it means to us. His shed blood gives us hope, gives us a future, gives us a reason to live.

Paul speaks of this hope in Romans.

> Romans 5:9-11—Much more then, being now justified by his blood, we shall be saved from wrath through him. For if, when we were enemies, we were reconciled to God by the death of his Son, much more, being reconciled, we shall be saved by his life. And not only so, but we also joy in God through our Lord Jesus Christ, by whom we have now received the atonement.

As saved children of God, we should joy in God and His Son, because through the shedding of Jesus' blood, we can have atonement! What a rich thought! What a priceless reality! All because of Christ's precious shed blood on Calvary.

The Precious Gospel

The gospel—that Christ died, was buried, rose again, and was seen of men—is also precious to God; for the power of the gospel is what reconciles sinful man to a holy God (1 Corinthians 15:3-5). The Apostle Paul recognized the gospel as a treasure given to mankind for the purpose of magnifying the Lord.

> 2 Corinthians 4:5-7—For we preach not ourselves, but Christ Jesus the Lord; and ourselves your servants for Jesus' sake. For God, who commanded the light to shine out of darkness, hath shined in our hearts, to give the light of the knowledge of the glory of God in the face of Jesus Christ. But we have this **treasure** in earthen vessels, that the excellency of the power may be of God, and not of us.

The word *treasure* in this passage means "wealth." To paraphrase, we have wealth here on earth through the gospel for the purpose of showing God's power. Without the gospel, we would be spiritually poor.

Albert Barnes writes that Paul "had spoken of the gospel, the knowledge of Jesus Christ, as full of glory, and infinitely precious. This rich blessing had been committed to him and his fellow labourers to dispense it to others and to diffuse it abroad."[1]

While the priceless blood of Christ was a precious act of love, the life-changing gospel is the precious message of God's love. Christ's shed blood and the gospel are God's greatest gift to the world (John 3:16), paving the way for us to be acceptable to Him.

Valuing the Treasure

We probably all agree that Christ's shed blood and the gospel message are priceless treasures that God values. We probably also agree that as Christians we should be grateful to God for our salvation. We would most likely go as far as to say that we do value Christ's blood and our salvation through believing the gospel. When asked how we value our salvation in Christ, we may use answers such as "I go to church," "I observe the Lord's Supper and thank the Lord for saving me," or "I tell others about the Bible."

These are all good answers and a good start to valuing the gospel treasure. What I found to be most helpful in valuing the gospel is a principle I learned from *Discipline of Grace* by Jerry Bridges. In a small chapter of his book, Bridges exhorts us to daily preach the gospel to ourselves.

> To preach the gospel to yourself, then, means that you continually face up to your own sinfulness and then flee to Jesus through faith in His shed blood and righteous life. It means that you appropriate, again by faith, the fact that Jesus fully satisfied the law of God, that He is your propitiation, and that God's holy wrath is no longer directed toward you . . . This is the gospel by which we were saved, and it is the gospel by which we must live every day of our Christian lives."[2]

We give value to the gospel by remembering God's grace and our sinfulness day by day, moment by moment. If we are not familiar with the gospel, we cannot preach it to ourselves, let alone explain it to others.

Evaluating My Treasure System

- If I find myself dreading another gospel message by my pastor, then I have failed in valuing the gospel.
- If I find myself struggling to remember key salvation verses to meditate on, then I have failed in valuing the gospel.
- If I do not claim God's promises concerning forgiveness, then I have failed in valuing the gospel.
- If I have forgotten that I am sinful and in need of God's grace each and every day, then I have failed in valuing the gospel.
- If I choose to continue in sin even after Christ saved me from the power of sin, then I have failed in valuing the gospel.
- If I find myself signing up for service opportunities so that I do not have to participate in the Lord's Supper, then I have failed in valuing the gospel.
- If I do not get excited about souls getting saved, then I have failed in valuing the gospel.

Treasuring the Treasure

A simple way that we can meditate on the gospel and the shed blood of Christ is by singing about them. Our songbooks are full of hymns and songs that take us back to the cross and to the power of the gospel. We can sing them, hum them, listen to them. By doing so, we are valuing the gospel treasure. But there are several ways we can revive the gospel in our lives beyond just through song. We can . . .

- write down verses about salvation on a 3x5 card and read the card a few times a day.
- write down in a journal what we are learning in our devotions.
- set an alarm on our watch or home clock to remind us to think about a certain Bible passage or lesson.
- task our computers so that every hour a reminder pops up on our screen to remind us to think of how the gospel changed us.
- share with friends what we are learning and rehearsing in our thoughts.
- make our mirrors talk to us in the morning by posting verses on them for us to review while we get ready for the day.
- play specific hymns that sparkle with the gospel message.
- scripturize our homes with verses so that our entire family can rehearse the good news of the gospel.
- share our salvation testimony with our children and speak of how our salvation changed us.
- read gospel tracts and evaluate them together as a family.

We need to rehearse and read the gospel to ourselves, to others, and to our families. Meditating on the gospel and Christ's shed blood on Calvary is essential to our remembering where we came from and where we are today because of Calvary.

Asking for help is crucial to our quest to treasure the blood and work of Christ. We need to beg God to give us a passion for the gospel, to give us gratitude for Christ's shed blood, to give us an understanding of how extraordinary the gift of salvation truly is, to remind us of our status before salvation, to encourage us to be courageous in sharing the gospel, to give us a yearning to study and know the meaning and power of the gospel, and to never, ever forget that God and His Son Jesus Christ did all of this because of love. We need God's help. We need His grace.

Possessing but Not Valuing
Just as many people discover that they have valuable antiques tucked away

in the corners of their dusty attics, damp basements, or cluttered garages, we, too, can possess a treasure without ever realizing how valuable it actually is.

As Christians we possess the gospel treasure. We are redeemed recipients of Christ's precious shed blood (Psalm 49:7-8). This treasure does not corrupt, does not fade, does not decrease in value, cannot be sold for a ransom, and cannot be stolen from us. The security of our treasure is outlined in John 10:27-29.

> My sheep hear my voice, and I know them, and they follow me: And I give unto them eternal life; and they shall never perish, neither shall any man pluck them out of my hand. My Father, which gave them me, is greater than all; and no man is able to pluck them out of my Father's hand.

Yet, we set this treasure aside in the corner of one of our storage rooms. We know better than to try to throw it away; after all, it is important fire insurance from hell. But we do not display it in our living rooms, we do not guard it against cynics, and we do not share it with others who we know would benefit from having the same treasure. Instead, we hoard the gospel and Christ's work in our lives as if we are ashamed of it, as if it is "old news," as if we believe it may fade if left in the sunlight too long, as if it has no value beyond fire insurance.

God clearly tells us in His Word that the gospel and the shed blood of His Son are precious treasures in His sight. They are the path to eternal life with God. If we want to emulate God's treasure system, the first and foremost treasure we need to begin to value is our salvation. Just as Paul reminded young Titus to never forget his position prior to salvation, to never forget God's mercy and kindness in saving him, and to proclaim this truth constantly, we, too, must treasure our salvation in Christ!

> Titus 3:3-8—For we ourselves also were sometimes foolish, disobedient, deceived, serving divers lusts and pleasures, living in malice and envy, hateful, and hating one another. But after that the kindness and love of God our Saviour toward man appeared, Not by works of righteousness which we have done, but according to his mercy he saved

us, by the washing of regeneration, and renewing of the Holy Ghost; Which he shed on us abundantly through Jesus Christ our Saviour; That being justified by his grace, we should be made heirs according to the hope of eternal life. This is a faithful saying, and these things I will that thou affirm constantly, that they which have believed in God might be careful to maintain good works. These things are good and profitable unto men.

Is the Blood of Christ Special?

We cannot deny that Christ's shed blood is special to God and should be a special treasure to the believer. Pastor Caswell A. Reeves compiled this list from Scripture of how the blood of Christ plays a major role in God's plan to redeem His Creation.[3]

Christ's blood is the agent God has chosen to bring us near to God.

Ephesians 2:13—But now in Christ Jesus ye who sometimes were far off are made nigh by the blood of Christ.

Christ's blood is the agent God has chosen to forgive us.

Colossians 1:14—In whom we have redemption through his blood, even the forgiveness of sins.

Christ's blood is the agent God has chosen to reconcile us to Himself.

Colossians 1:20—And, having made peace through the blood of his cross, by him to reconcile all things unto himself; by him, I say, whether they be things in earth, or things in heaven.

Christ's blood is the agent God has chosen to eternally redeem us.

Hebrews 9:12—Neither by the blood of goats and calves, but by his own blood he entered in once into the holy place, having obtained eternal redemption for us.

Christ's blood is the agent God has chosen to purify and sanctify us for service.

Hebrews 9:13-14—For if the blood of bulls and of goats, and the ashes of an heifer sprinkling the unclean, sanctifieth to the purifying of the flesh: How much more shall the blood of Christ, who through the eternal Spirit offered himself without spot to God, purge your conscience from dead works to serve the living God?

Christ's blood is the agent God has chosen to give us entrance into the holiest.

Hebrews 10:19—Having therefore, brethren, boldness to enter into the holiest by the blood of Jesus.

Christ's blood is the agent God has given to cleanse us from sin.

1 John 1:7—But if we walk in the light, as he is in the light, we have fellowship one with another, and the blood of Jesus Christ his Son cleanseth us from all sin.

Christ's blood is the agent God has chosen to make white the believer's heavenly robe.

Revelation 7:14—And I said unto him, Sir, thou knowest. And he said to me, These are they which came out of great tribulation, and have washed their robes, and made them white in the blood of the Lamb.

Christ's blood is the agent God has chosen for believers to overcome the devil.

Revelation 12:9-11—And the great dragon was cast out, that old serpent, called the Devil, and Satan, which deceiveth the whole world: he was cast out into the earth, and his angels were cast out with him. And I heard a loud voice saying in heaven, Now is come salvation, and strength, and the kingdom of our God, and the power of his Christ: for the accuser of our brethren is cast down, which accused them before our God day and night. And they overcame him by the blood of the Lamb, and by the word of their testimony; and they loved not their lives unto the death.

The precious blood of Christ is a valuable fountain that should flow in and through our conversation and life. May we treasure this gift each and every day of our lives.

Nothing But the Blood

What can wash away my sin?
Nothing but the blood of Jesus;
What can make me whole again?
Nothing but the blood of Jesus.

Oh! precious is the flow
That makes me white as snow;
No other fount I know,
Nothing but the blood of Jesus.

This is all my hope and peace
Nothing but the blood of Jesus;
This is all my righteousness
Nothing but the blood of Jesus.

Oh! precious is the flow
That makes me white as snow;
No other fount I know,
Nothing but the blood of Jesus.

--Robert Lowry[1]

THE WORTH OF THIS TREASURE

1 Peter 1:18-19

Forasmuch as ye know that ye were not redeemed with corruptible things, as silver and gold, from your vain conversation received by tradition from your fathers; But with the precious blood of Christ, as of a lamb without blemish and without spot.

- Its Origin: God gave His only begotten Son because of His love
- Its Purpose: For our salvation through faith in Christ
- Its Potential: Eternal life

What keeps me from valuing the blood and work of Christ? Pride; forgetfulness.

Epilogue
The System's Foundation

The gospel is the foundation of God's value system. It is the cornerstone of God's checkbook. It is the standard by which all other treasures should be measured. The gospel is God's most precious treasure that He wants us to possess and then to share with others. This treasure is not meant to be hidden or locked away. It cannot be sold. It cannot be bought, for the price has already been paid. A priceless gospel can only be paid with a priceless gift—Jesus' precious blood. Because of this truth, I asked readers to visit chapter 10 twice before finishing this book. All of God's treasures are rooted in the gospel. We need to wrap our minds and souls around the meaning and message of the gospel. Valuing the gospel is an important step; and I have inserted in Appendix C a copy-and-use resource that can easily fit in a Bible, purse, wallet, or pocket to remind each of us of the importance of the gospel. All of the other heavenly treasures revolve around God and His gospel.

On this note, I end this study on God's treasure system similar to the way I began. In the first chapter, I encouraged my readers to start their treasure hunt into God's treasure system by first learning to value God by spending time with Him. By spending time with God and meditating on what He says in His Word, God's values will begin to become intrinsic to us. His values soon become our values. I also encouraged readers to not stop studying God's treasures. Many more treasures can be found from searching God's treasure map, the Bible. Although this book ends here, I hope and pray my readers keep discovering valuable nuggets of truth.

I want to adorn my soul with the gospel and its benefits, and I want to live in such a way that makes others want to adorn their lives with the same precious gospel. I trust we love the gospel and then live the gospel on a daily basis. God's treasures are our claim to cherish. May we learn to value what God values.

To God be the glory!

Why are these items a part of God's treasure system?	
A Virtuous Woman	Virtue (an inner strength) is a testimony of God's grace and my dependence on God. Others will see it and want it, giving me opportunity to point them to Christ.
The Trials of Our Faith	Trials are designed to draw me closer to God as I lean on Him. They require me to trust Him. As others witness my biblical response to these trials, I can share with them my hope in Christ.
Marriage	Marriage represents the union and sacrifice of Christ to the church. It is a picture of the gospel. By valuing my marriage, I communicate the gospel to others.
God's Promises	Promises from God's Word proclaim God's faithfulness and cause me to hope in God for His sustenance and grace. I can depend on these promises and share this confidence with others.
His Lovingkindness	God's lovingkindness is evidence that there is a God Who loves me unconditionally. This thought drives me to Him. This truth compels me to share its benefits with others.
The Death of a Saint	My death is the final act that places me in God's presence forevermore. My trust in the gospel makes heaven my home.
A Meek and Quiet Spirit	This heart ornamentation that is founded on what I know about God draws others to Him. The resulting behavior causes me to become a walking gospel tract.
Wisdom	Wisdom requires me to know and fear God, for I cannot have wisdom until I have learned Who God is and who I am. A relationship with Christ is a must, and this begins at salvation.
The Work of Christ	Trusting in the shed blood of Christ to redeem me is the only way I can be cleansed from sin in order to live eternally with God.

Appendix A

> *To Entertain* means "to receive into the house and treat with hospitality, either at the table only, or with lodging also"

Spiritual Application

As a Christian, Christ resides in my heart and becomes a full-time resident in my life. How do I receive Him? Do I welcome His company? Is the fellowship sweet around the table?

Scriptural Principles

1 Corinthians 3:16—Know ye not that ye are the temple of God, and that the Spirit of God dwelleth in you?

2 Corinthians 6:16—And what agreement hath the temple of God with idols? for ye are the temple of the living God; as God hath said, I will dwell in them, and walk in them; and I will be their God, and they shall be my people.

Revelation 3:20—Behold, I stand at the door, and knock: if any man hear my voice, and open the door, I will come in to him, and will sup with him, and he with me.

> *To Entertain* means "to treat with conversation; to amuse or instruct by discourse, to engage the attention and retain the company of one by agreeable conversation"

Spiritual Application

Although I am unworthy to instruct the Lord through my discourse, I am obligated to engage and retain Christ's company as we converse together throughout the day. Do I talk with the Lord? Do I amuse the Lord with my thoughts and feelings, or do I grieve Him? Furthermore, do I find His words to be provoking? Do I find the preaching and presentations of God's Word amusing or boring? Do I look forward to and participate in conversations with the Lord?

Scriptural Principles

1 Thessalonians 5:17—Pray without ceasing.

Psalm 63:5-6—My soul shall be satisfied as with marrow and fatness; and my mouth shall praise thee with joyful lips: When I remember thee upon my bed, and meditate on thee in the night watches.

Psalm 55:17—Evening, and morning, and at noon, will I pray, and cry aloud: and he shall hear my voice.

Luke 24:32—And they said one to another, Did not our heart burn within us, while he talked with us by the way, and while he opened to us the scriptures?

> *To Entertain* means "to keep, hold, or maintain in the mind with favor; to reserve in the mind; to harbor; to cherish"

Spiritual Application

As God's child, do I favor the things of God? Do I work hard at maintaining holiness? Do I strive to make God happy, and do I see that striving as favorable (honorable)? Do I meditate on the things of God? Do I cherish and desire to keep close to me the things that God declares valuable? Am I delighting in Him?

Scriptural Principles

Philippians 4:8—Finally, brethren, whatsoever things are true, whatsoever things are honest, whatsoever things are just, whatsoever things are pure, whatsoever things are lovely, whatsoever things are of good report; if there be any virtue, and if there be any praise, think on these things.

Psalm 73:25—Whom have I in heaven but thee? and there is none upon earth that I desire beside thee.

Ecclesiastes 12:13—Let us hear the conclusion of the whole matter: Fear God, and keep his commandments: for this is the whole duty of man.

> *To Entertain* means "to please; to amuse"

Spiritual Application

Just as I should delight in what God is doing in my life, God should be able to delight in my life because of my choices to honor and obey Him. Do I please Him? Do I delight (find amusement) in His Word? What pleases me the most? Am I making choices that are well-pleasing to God? Is God entertained by my life or nauseated by my life?

Scriptural Principles

Psalm 1:2—But his delight is in the law of the LORD; and in his law doth he meditate day and night.

Psalm 119:48—My hands also will I lift up unto thy commandments, which I have loved; and I will meditate in thy statutes.

Psalm 143:5—I remember the days of old; I meditate on all thy works; I muse on the work of thy hands.

Psalm 27:4—One thing have I desired of the LORD, that will I seek after; that I may dwell in the house of the LORD, all the days of my life, to behold the beauty of the LORD, and to enquire in his temple.

To *Entertain* means "to treat; to supply with provisions and lodging"

Spiritual Application

God has graciously given His only Son to die for me. What can I give back to Him? What can I offer Christ? Everything I offer will be filthy, but what I can do is say yes to Him when He asks me to serve, to obey, to believe, to honor, to speak, to pray, and to forgive. Am I treating others with the same graciousness God treated me? Am I giving with a cheerful heart? Am I supplying my fellow brethren with encouraging words and timely provisions?

Scriptural Principles

2 Corinthians 9:7—Every man according as he purposeth in his heart, so let him give; not grudgingly, or of necessity: for God loveth a cheerful giver.

Ephesians 4:32—And be ye kind one to another, tenderhearted, forgiving one another, even as God for Christ's sake hath forgiven you.

Romans 4:20—He staggered not at the promise of God through unbelief; but was strong in faith, giving glory to God.

Hebrews 13:2—Be not forgetful to entertain strangers: for thereby some have entertained angels unawares.

Appendix B

A Parallel of God's Kindness

My pastor paralleled Joseph's goodness to his brothers with how God shows His goodness to us. The comparison is powerful and was helpful in my understanding God's lovingkindness in my own life.

Joseph's Brothers' Rescue

Genesis 42:1-2—Now when Jacob saw that there was corn in Egypt, Jacob said unto his sons, Why do ye look one upon another? And he said, Behold, I have heard that there is corn in Egypt: get you down thither, and buy for us from thence; that we may live, and not die.

Poverty brought Jacob and his family to Joseph. Jacob's choice was either to starve in Canaan or live in Egypt.

My Rescue

Romans 7:9 and 6:23—For I was alive without the law once: but when the commandment came, sin revived, and I died. For the wages of sin is death; but the gift of God is eternal life through Jesus Christ our Lord.

My sin brings me to God. My choice is either to die in sin or live with God.

Joseph's Brothers' Rescue

Genesis 42:8—And Joseph knew his brethren, but they knew not him.

Jacob's sons did not recognize Joseph, their rescuer and brother; but Joseph knew his brothers.

My Rescue

Psalm 139:1-4—O LORD, thou hast searched me, and known me. Thou knowest my downsitting and mine uprising, thou understandest my thought afar off. Thou compassest my path and my lying down, and art acquainted with all my ways. For there is not a word in my tongue, but, lo, O LORD, thou knowest it altogether.

God knows me even though I don't know Him or recognize Him.

Joseph's Brothers' Rescue

Genesis 42:21—And they [Joseph's brothers] said one to another, We are verily guilty concerning our brother [Joseph], in that we saw the anguish of his soul, when he besought us, and we would not hear; therefore is this distress come upon us.

Jacob's sons remembered their sins and felt guilt and distress as a result of those remembered sins.

My Rescue

Romans 7:5, 23-24—For when we were in the flesh, the motions of sins, which were by the law, did work in our members to bring forth fruit unto death. But I see another law in my members, warring against the law of my mind, and bringing me into captivity to the law of sin which is in my members. O wretched man that I am! who shall deliver me from the body of this death?

My conscience and my memories remind me I am a sinner, guilty and seemingly without hope.

Joseph's Brothers' Rescue

Genesis 43:16-18—And when Joseph saw Benjamin with them, he said to the ruler of his house, Bring these men home, and slay, and make ready; for these men shall dine with me at noon. And the man did as Joseph bade; and the man brought the men into Joseph's house. And the men were afraid, because they were brought into Joseph's house; and they said, Because of the money that was returned in our sacks at the first time are we brought in; that he may seek occasion against us, and fall upon us, and take us for bondmen, and our asses.

My Rescue

Psalm 106:7-14—Our fathers understood not thy wonders in Egypt; they remembered not the multitude of thy mercies; but provoked him at the sea, even at the Red sea. Nevertheless he saved them for his name's sake, that he might make his mighty power to be known. He rebuked the Red sea also, and it was dried up: so he led them through the depths, as through the wilderness. And he saved them from the hand of him that hated them, and redeemed them from the hand of the enemy. And the waters covered their enemies: there was not one of

Joseph's Brothers' Rescue

Joseph's brothers questioned Joseph's kindness. They assumed that Joseph's motives were evil.

My Rescue

them left. Then believed they his words; they sang his praise. They soon forgat his works; they waited not for his counsel: But lusted exceedingly in the wilderness, and tempted God in the desert.

Just as the children of Israel questioned God's motives and goodness, so I question God's working in my life.

Joseph's Brothers' Rescue

Genesis 43:29-30—And he lifted up his eyes, and saw his brother Benjamin, his mother's son, and said, Is this your younger brother, of whom ye spake unto me? And he said, God be gracious unto thee, my son. And Joseph made haste; for his bowels did yearn upon his brother: and he sought where to weep; and he entered into his chamber, and wept there.

Joseph wept for his brothers. He yearned [deeply affected with a passion] for them.

My Rescue

Matthew 26:37-43 And he took with him Peter and the two sons of Zebedee, and began to be sorrowful and very heavy. Then saith he unto them, My soul is exceeding sorrowful, even unto death: tarry ye here, and watch with me. And he went a little further, and fell on his face, and prayed, saying, O my Father, if it be possible, let this cup pass from me: nevertheless not as I will, but as thou wilt.
Luke 19:41-42—And when [Jesus] was come near, he beheld the city, and wept over it, Saying, If thou hadst known, even thou, at least in this thy day, the things which belong unto thy peace!

Jesus weeps for His own. He yearns for my fellowship.

Joseph's Brothers' Rescue

Genesis 43:32-33—And they set on for him by himself, and for them by themselves, and for the Egyptians, which did eat with him, by themselves: because the Egyptians might not eat bread with the Hebrews; for that is an abomination unto the Egyptians. And they sat before him, the firstborn according to his birthright, and the youngest according to his youth: and the men marvelled one at another.

Joseph arranged his brothers at the table in birth order, and Joseph's brothers marveled at how Joseph would have known them and their customs so well.

My Rescue

Psalm 139:15-17—My substance was not hid from thee, when I was made in secret, and curiously wrought in the lowest parts of the earth. Thine eyes did see my substance, yet being unperfect; and in thy book all my members were written, which in continuance were fashioned, when as yet there was none of them. How precious also are thy thoughts unto me, O God! how great is the sum of them!

David marveled, and I marvel, too, that God knows me and thinks precious thoughts about me

Joseph's Brothers' Rescue

Genesis 45:1-3—Then Joseph could not refrain himself before all them that stood by him; and he cried, Cause every man to go out from me. And there stood no man with him, while Joseph made himself known unto his brethren. And he wept aloud: and the Egyptians and the house of Pharaoh heard. And Joseph said unto his brethren, I am Joseph; doth my father yet live? And his brethren could not answer him; for they were troubled at his presence.

My Rescue

Isaiah 6:5—Then said I, Woe is me! for I am undone; because I am a man of unclean lips, and I dwell in the midst of a people of unclean lips: for mine eyes have seen the King, the LORD of hosts.

Job 42:5-6—I have heard of thee by the hearing of the ear: but now mine eye seeth thee. Wherefore I abhor myself, and repent in dust and ashes.

Joseph's Brothers' Rescue

Joseph made himself known to his brethren, and Joseph's presence troubled them [caused alarm and agitation].

My Rescue

Seeing God's holiness causes me to hate the sin in my life. If I don't hate the sin in my life, then I haven't seen God for Who He is.

Joseph's Brothers' Rescue

Genesis 45:9-11—Haste ye, and go up to my father, and say unto him, Thus saith thy son Joseph, God hath made me lord of all Egypt: come down unto me, tarry not: And thou shalt dwell in the land of Goshen, and thou shalt be near unto me, thou, and thy children, and thy children's children, and thy flocks, and thy herds, and all that thou hast: And there will I nourish thee; for yet there are five years of famine; lest thou, and thy household, and all that thou hast, come to poverty.

Joseph desired fellowship and wanted to provide for his family. He extended grace to his murderous brothers.

My Rescue

Revelation 3:19-20—As many as I love, I rebuke and chasten: be zealous therefore, and repent. Behold, I stand at the door, and knock: if any man hear my voice, and open the door, I will come in to him, and will sup with him, and he with me.

Ephesians 2:4-7—But God, who is rich in mercy, for his great love wherewith he loved us, Even when we were dead in sins, hath quickened us together with Christ, (by grace ye are saved;) And hath raised us up together, and made us sit together in heavenly places in Christ Jesus: That in the ages to come he might shew the exceeding riches of his grace in his kindness toward us through Christ Jesus.

God desires my fellowship and does provide for me as a Father provides for His child's every need. He extends grace to me at salvation and beyond.

Joseph's Brothers' Rescue

My Rescue

Genesis 47:11-12—And Joseph placed his father and his brethren, and gave them a possession in the land of Egypt, in the best of the land, in the land of Rameses, as Pharaoh had commanded. And Joseph nourished his father, and his brethren, and all his father's household, with bread, according to their families.

Joseph and his family experienced restored fellowship, but Joseph also provided the very best for his family. Joseph sustained his family.

James 1:17—Every good gift and every perfect gift is from above, and cometh down from the Father of lights, with whom is no variableness, neither shadow of turning.

John 14:1-3—Let not your heart be troubled: ye believe in God, believe also in me. In my Father's house are many mansions: if it were not so, I would have told you. I go to prepare a place for you. And if I go and prepare a place for you, I will come again, and receive you unto myself; that where I am, there ye may be also.

Not only do I receive the very best here on earth, but also God is preparing the very best for me in heaven. He sustains me each day and throughout eternity.

Appendix C

Lest I Forget the Gospel's Value in My Life

God's Treasure System by Shannon B. Steuerwald

God's holiness exposes my sin. My sin separates me from God and sends me to hell. God's love outlines a rescue plan through His Son Jesus Christ. When I believe in Jesus' death and resurrection as my Propitiator and confess my sins to God, I experience God's righteous deliverance from an eternal death in hell. God's justice demanded blameless blood to be shed for my justification. His mercy provided a Lamb when I deserved the cross. As His child, I now have full and bold access to God's power, which includes His Spirit and His strength to overcome my deepest fears and sinful struggles, as well as His protective arms to shield me from the satanic darts that I cannot handle. On a daily basis, I feel God's kindness toward me as He cares for my every need and even extends blessings beyond my hopes and expectations. He does all of this because He is for me. He is my Father, my God, my Creator. And because I am His child, He graciously continues to give to me what I do not deserve, including forgiveness of sin, as I remember all that He has done for me and humbly acknowledge that He is the God of holiness, love, righteousness, justice, power, and kindness. Contrary to what my sinful nature tells me, I am inadequate to be or do anything without God. Yet, God, Who is the same yesterday, today, and forever, faithfully fulfills His every promise to me. Therefore, I can and must trust Him for everything He places and performs in my life. This trust and obedience to God brings me joy unspeakable and compels me to worship Him for Who He is and how He has saved me.

Appendix D

Treasuring God's Kindness	
Treasure Principle	**Applying the Treasure Principle**
Proclaim God's Kindness	When was the last time I shared with my spouse, my children, my co-workers, my Sunday school class, my pastor, or my friends how God has been kind to me? What can I do today to better treasure God's kindness in my life?
Thank God for His Kindness	When was the last time I thanked God, whether through private prayer or during corporate prayer, for the kindness He shed on me? Do I thank God for the blessings and trials in my life knowing that both are a result of His goodness in my life? Do I acknowledge God's kindness by thanking Him for it? What can I do today to better treasure God's kindness in my life?
Think about God's Kindness	Do I ponder God's kindness throughout the day? Do I think about and meditate on how He has been kind to me. Have I spent some time writing down all of the ways that God has shown His kindness to me? What can I do today to better treasure God's kindness in my life?
Regard God's Kindness	Do I see the different events, trials, blessings, and people in my life as acts of God's kindness in my life? Do I regard the details of God's creation as good? Is my heart hearing God's kindness so that I can better respond to His working in my life? What can I do today to better treasure God's kindness in my life?
Love God's Kindness	Am I practicing loving God's kindness by loving others? Do I show kindness to my brothers and sisters in Christ? Have I asked God to give me a deeper love for others? Am I willing to forgive others as Christ forgave me? Do I display God's love to others by the way I love? What can I do today to better treasure God's kindness in my life?
Trust God's Kindness	Do I lean on God's kindness during hard times, or do I blame God for the hard times? Do I believe that God is always good and never bad? Am I displaying my trust in God's leadership and love for me by obeying Him? What can I do today to better treasure God's kindness in my life?

Appendix E

As Unto the Lord

Does my submission to my husband compare well to
how Scripture tells the church to submit to the Lord?

How should the church view Christ?

He is Pre-eminent.
Colossians 1:18—And he [Christ] is the head of the body, the church: who is the beginning, the firstborn from the dead; that in all things he might have the preeminence.

Is my husband listed at the top of my priority list? Is he ranked first in my family? Would my children agree with my answer?

He is the Savior.
Ephesians 5:23—For the husband is the head of the wife, even as Christ is the head of the church: and he is the saviour of the body.

Do I see my husband as my protector? Do I allow my husband to make decisions for our family, or do I overstep?

He is the Head.
Ephesians 5:23—For the husband is the head of the wife, even as Christ is the head of the church: and he is the saviour of the body.

Do I allow my husband to lead at his pace? Am I content, or do I complain about the man God has given me?

He is One with the church.
Ephesians 5:30—For we [the church] are members of his body, of his flesh, and of his bones.

Do I complement my husband? Are we living separate lives? Do we have separate goals? Is he my companion?

How should the church obey Christ?

With full faith
I need to obey my husband's decisions even when they don't make sense to me.

Hebrews 11:6
Isaiah 55:8-9

With joy
I need to delight in obeying my husband.

John 15:10-11
Psalm 40:8

With knowledge
I need to know my husband's wishes and honor them. I need to work diligently at knowing him.

Proverbs 2:1-5
Colossians 1:10
> "There should be such mutual love and confidence, that the known wish of the husband should be a law to the wife; and that the known desires of the wife should be the rule which he would approve. A perfect government is that where the known wish of the lawgiver is a sufficient rule to the subject. Such is the government of heaven; and a family on earth should approximate as nearly as possible to that."[1]

With reverence
I need to respect and be "in awe" of my husband.

Proverbs 23:17
Proverbs 1:28-33

With love
I need to love my husband.

1 John 5:2

With thankfulness
I need to appreciate and show gratitude to my husband and his leadership.

Colossians 2:7
Colossians 3:17

[1]Barnes, Albert. *Albert Barnes' Notes on the New Testament*. Ephesians 5:22. Electronic Version.

Appendix F

A Summary of the Treasures

Chapter 2: A Virtuous Woman

Proverbs 31:10—Who can find a virtuous woman? for her price is far above rubies.

   The Worth of This Treasure
   - Its Origin: From God
   - Its Purpose: To help a woman be a better keeper of her home
   - Its Potential: A happy family; a trusting husband

What keeps me from valuing virtue and the virtuous woman? Trying to be virtuous on my own (pride; self-ambition); not recognizing that God values a virtuous woman.

Chapter 3: The Trials of Our Faith

1 Peter 1:6-7—Wherein ye greatly rejoice, though now for a season, if need be, ye are in heaviness through manifold temptations: That the trial of your faith, being much more precious than of gold that perisheth, though it be tried with fire, might be found unto praise and honour and glory at the appearing of Jesus Christ.

   The Worth of This Treasure
   - Its Origin: From God
   - Its Purpose: To help draw one closer to God; to be purified
   - Its Potential: A sweeter relationship with God for His glory

What keeps me from valuing the trials of my faith? My sinful responses, my lack of trust, my unbelief.

Chapter 4: Marriage

Hebrews 13:4—Marriage is honourable in all, and the bed undefiled: but whoremongers and adulterers God will judge.

   The Worth of This Treasure
   - Its Origin: Instituted by God; obtained the minute we say, "I do."
   - Its Purpose: To represent the union of Christ and the church

- Its Potential: Companionship; help; children and family that live forever

What keeps me from valuing marriage? My choices; my poor belief system; my listening to and reading secular advice.

Chapter 5: God's Promises

2 Peter 1:4—Whereby are given unto us exceeding great and precious promises: that by these ye might be partakers of the divine nature, having escaped the corruption that is in the world through lust.

The Worth of This Treasure
- Its Origin: From God; we partake by faith through divine grace
- Its Purpose: For God to show Himself faithful to us; so we could experience the abundance of God's storehouse of love
- Its Potential: We become partakers of the divine nature

What keeps me from valuing God's promises? Not believing; not meditating; not knowing.

Chapter 6: His Lovingkindness

Psalm 36:7—How excellent is thy lovingkindness, O God! therefore the children of men put their trust under the shadow of thy wings.

The Worth of This Treasure
- Its Origin: God is love, and God loves us.
- Its Purpose: To draw us to God; an outward display of God's love
- Its Potential: I am a recipient of God's goodness which is limitless

What keeps me from valuing His lovingkindness? My pride as I move away from God's protection and power.

Chapter 7: The Death of a Saint

Psalm 116:15—Precious in the sight of the LORD is the death of his saints.

The Worth of This Treasure
- Its Origin: Everyone will die, but not everyone is a saint. A person becomes a saint at salvation.
- Its Purpose: God's way of bringing me home to heaven and reminding those on earth that life is just a vapor
- Its Potential: Heaven; eternal rest; earthly comfort

What keeps me from valuing the death of a saint? Sorrowing without hope; improper thinking.

Chapter 8: A Meek and Quiet Spirit

1 Peter 3:4—But let it be the hidden man of the heart, in that which is not corruptible, even the ornament of a meek and quiet spirit, which is in the sight of God of great price.

The Worth of This Treasure
- Its Origin: Found in the inner man when I emulate Christ and His Word
- Its Purpose: To draw others to Christ; to make the gospel sparkle
- Its Potential: Improved relationship with husband; incorruptible beauty

What keeps me from valuing a meek and quiet spirit? Unbelief; pride; misaligned priorities; selfishness.

Chapter 9: Wisdom

Proverbs 3:13-15—Happy is the man that findeth wisdom, and the man that getteth understanding. For the merchandise of it is better than the merchandise of silver, and the gain thereof than fine gold. She is more precious than rubies: and all the things thou canst desire are not to be compared unto her.

The Worth of This Treasure
- Its Origin: From fearing God and by wanting it
- Its Purpose: To be pure, peaceable, gentle, submissive, merciful, full of good works; not wavering

- Its Potential: Happiness; long days; riches; honor; pleasantness; peace

What keeps me from valuing wisdom? Not fearing; not searching; not asking.

Chapter 10: The Work of Christ

1 Peter 1:18-19—Forasmuch as ye know that ye were not redeemed with corruptible things, as silver and gold, from your vain conversation received by tradition from your fathers; But with the precious blood of Christ, as of a lamb without blemish and without spot.

The Worth of This Treasure
- Its Origin: God gave His only begotten Son because of His love
- Its Purpose: For our salvation through faith in Christ
- Its Potential: Eternal life

What keeps me from valuing the blood and work of Christ? Pride; forgetfulness.

Notes

Chapter 2

1. Webster, Noah. *Webster's 1828 Dictionary*. "Virtue."

2. Strong, James. *The Exhaustive Concordance of the Bible*. Nashville, TN: Holman Bible Publishers. Greek #703, arête.

3. Ibid, Hebrew #2428, chayil.

4. Edwards, Miall D. *International Standard Bible Encyclopedia*. "Virtue." Logos Bible Software.

5. Lockyer, Herbert. *All the Women of the Bible*. Grand Rapids, MI: Zondervan Publishing House. Page 272.

6. In an attempt to be as practical as possible, I sometimes feel that I am overemphasizing what I can do to change and failing to highlight what God does in my life. I struggle as a writer and teacher to know best how to balance this equation. I remember hearing a speaker say, "Pray as if everything depends on God; do as if everything depends on you." I don't like this quote because my life needs to communicate dependence on God first and foremost. Being or becoming virtuous is only possible because of God's grace. The very desire to be virtuous is from God. In the midst of trying to give you practical helps in becoming virtuous, my prayer is that you first start by praying and asking God for His grace as you humbly admit that being or becoming virtuous is impossible without Him.

Chapter 3

1. Berg, Jim Dr. *Taking Time to Quiet Your Soul*. Greenville, SC: BJU Press, 2005. Page 51.

2. Hendricks, Howard and Bob Phillips. *Values and Virtues*. Quoted William R. Inge. Sisters, OR: Multnomah Books, 1997. Page 115.

3. Cheaney, Janie B. "Walking on Air." WORLD. April 22, 2006, page 51.

4. To properly understand Romans 8:28, one needs to know the meaning of good. Verse 29 of Romans 8 defines good: "to be conformed to the image of His Son." God is orchestrating the trials and blessings in my life to draw me closer to Him, to be more like Him. Therefore, the trials and blessings are good. Our response communicates whether we see and value the trials and blessings as good treasures from God.

5. Crosby, Fanny J. "To God Be the Glory." This hymn can be found in almost every major hymnal.

Chapter 5

1. Spurgeon, Charles. *Morning and Evening*. July 13. Psalm 56:9.
2. Webster, Noah. *Webster's 1828 Dictionary*. "Promise."
3. Tozer, A. W. *The Quotable Tozer II*. Camp Hill, PA: Christian Publications, 1997. Pages 157-158. This quotation was originally printed in Tozer's book entitled *The Tozer Pulpit Set*, Volume 1, Book 3.
4. Harper, Doulas. Online Etymology Dictionary. 2001. www.etymonline.com. Accessed February 1, 2007.
5. Spurgeon, Charles. *The Treasury of David*. Volume 1. Peobody, MA: Hendrickson Publishers. Psalm 63:1-3.
6. Nelson, Greg, James Isaac Elliott, and Phil McHugh. "You Can't Stand on Promises." Shepherd's Fold Music (a division of EMI Christian Music Publishing), 1982.

Chapter 6

1. *Harper's Bible Dictionary*. "Lovingkindness." Logos Version. Page 581.
2. Brown, Joan Winmill. *Wings of Joy*. "What More Can You Ask" by Helen Steiner Rice. Minneapolis, MN: World Wide Publications, 1977. Pages 18-19.

Chapter 7

1. Berg, Jim. *Taking Time to Quiet Your Soul*. Greenville, SC: BJU Press, 2005. Page 58.
2. Spurgeon, Charles. *Treasury of David*. Psalm 144:3.
3. Bennett, William J., editor. *The Book of Virtues*. "Faith." Pages 769-770. Poem entitled "Nearer Home" by Phoebe Cary.

Chapter 8

1. Finlayson, R. *The Pulpit Commentary*. "Homilies on 1 Peter 3." Rio, WI: Ages Software, Inc., 2001. Page 69.
2. Thomson, J.R. *The Pulpit Commentary*. "Homilies on 1 Peter 3." Rio, WI: Ages Software, Inc., 2001. Pages 39-40.
3. Finlayson, R. *The Pulpit Commentary*. "Homilies on 1 Peter 3." Rio, WI: Ages Software, Inc., 2001. Page 68.
4. Burkitt, William. *William Burkitt's Expository Notes*. 1 Peter 3:3.
5. *The Bible Knowledge Commentary*. Volume 2, Page 848. 1 Peter 3:3-4. Logos Bible Software.

6. Vine, W. E. *Vine's Complete Expository Dictionary of Old and New Testament Words*. "Meek, Meekness." Nashville, TN: Thomas Nelson Publishers, 1996. Page 401.

7. Strong, James. *The Exhaustive Concordance of the Bible*. Nashville, TN: Holman Bible Publishers. Greek #2272, hesuchios.

8. Mahaney, Carolyn and Nicole Mahaney Whitacre. *Girl Talk*. Wheaton, IL: Crossway Books, 2005. Page 27.

Chapter 9

1. Hendricks, Howard and Bob Phillips. *Values and Virtues*. Quoted Benjamin Franklin. Sisters, OR: Multnomah Books, 1997. Page 271.

2. Webster, Noah. *Webster's 1828 Dictionary*. "Wisdom."

Chapter 10

1. Barnes, Albert. *Albert Barnes' Notes on the New Testament*. 2 Corinthians 4:5-7.

2. Bridges, Jerry. *The Discipline of Grace*. Colorado Springs, CO: Navpress, 1994. Pages 58-59.

3. Reeves, Pastor Caswell. "Is the Blood of Christ Special?" October 2006. Used by permission.

4. Lowry, Robert. "Nothing But the Blood." This hymn can be found in almost every major hymnal.

Also Available by Shannon B. Steuerwald

A Proverb a Day Keeps the Naughties Away
Shannon Steuerwald

Being naughty is a serious matter! Unfortunately, today's use of the word has made being "naughty" seem cute and elementary. By God's standard, being naughty has nothing to do with our age but has everything to do with how we are and how we behave. With the help of Wisey Worm's Bible reading guidelines, calendar, and memory cards found in this devotional, you can begin to form healthy patterns that move you farther away from being naughty and draw you closer to knowing God. Parents can use this devotional during family devotions to teach their children how to read and apply Scripture, teachers and students can use this devotional as a supplement to school curriculum to help formulate a solid devotional schedule, and individuals can use this devotional in their personal walk with God.

From Scrawny to Brawny
Shannon Steuerwald
Illustrated by Sarah Forsythe

Being scrawny is never fun! For Wisey, being scrawny is all he ever knew until one day he discovers the secret to becoming brawny. Wisey, encouraged by his friends Squirm and Pudge, determines to unlock the mystery of From Scrawny to Brawny.

Shannon's goal in writing this children's book was to bring glory to God by presenting an entertaining, true-to-life story that naturally paralleled our spiritual lives in Christ. With the help of Sarah's artistic talent that captures Wisey's adventures, you have a children's book that will appeal to children while teaching worthwhile truths.

Ordering Information
www.ironwood.org
760.257.3503

Ironwood
49191 Cherokee Road
Newberry Springs, CA 92365